Library of
Davidson College

CONCILIUM
Religion in the Eighties

CONCILIUM

Editorial Directors

Giuseppe Alberigo	Bologna	Italy
Gregory Baum	Toronto	Canada
Leonardo Boff	Petrópolis	Brazil
Antoine van den Boogaard	Nijmegen	The Netherlands
Paul Brand	Ankeveen	The Netherlands
Marie-Dominique Chenu OP	Paris	France
John Coleman SJ	Berkeley, Ca.	USA
Mary Collins OSB	Washington	USA
Yves Congar OP	Paris	France
Mariasusai Dhavamony SJ	Rome	Italy
Christian Duquoc OP	Lyons	France
Virgil Elizondo	San Antonio, Texas	USA
Casiano Floristán	Madrid	Spain
Claude Geffré OP	Paris	France
Norbert Greinacher	Tübingen	West Germany
Gustavo Gutiérrez	Lima	Peru
Peter Huizing SJ	Nijmegen	The Netherlands
Bas van Iersel SMM	Nijmegen	The Netherlands
Jean-Pierre Jossua OP	Paris	France
Hans Küng	Tübingen	West Germany
Nicholas Lash	Cambridge	Great Britain
René Laurentin	Paris	France
Johannes-Baptist Metz	Münster	West Germany
Dietmar Mieth	Düdingen	Switzerland
Jürgen Moltmann	Tübingen	West Germany
Roland Murphy OCarm	Durham, NC	USA
Jacques Pohier OP	Paris	France
David Power OMI	Washington, DC	USA
Karl Rahner SJ	Munich	West Germany
Luigi Sartori	Padua	Italy
Edward Schillebeeckx OP	Nijmegen	The Netherlands
Elisabeth Schüssler Fiorenza	Hyattsville, Ind.	USA
David Tracy	Chicago	USA
Knut Walf	Nijmegen	The Netherlands
Anton Weiler	Nijmegen	The Netherlands
John Zizioulas	Glasgow	Great Britain

Lay Specialist Advisers

José Luis Aranguren	Madrid/Santa Barbara, Ca.	Spain/USA
Luciano Caglioti	Rome	Italy
August Wilhelm von Eiff	Bonn	West Germany
Paulo Freire	Perdizes, São Paulo	Brazil
Harald Weinrich	Munich	West Germany

Concilium 158 (8/1982): Ecumenism

THE RIGHT TO DISSENT

Edited by
Hans Küng
and
Jürgen Moltmann

English Language Editor
Marcus Lefébure

T. & T. CLARK LTD.　　　THE SEABURY PRESS
Edinburgh　　　　　　　　New York

Copyright © 1982, by Stichting Concilium, T. & T. Clark Ltd. and The Seabury Press Inc. All rights reserved. Nothing contained in this publication shall be multiplied and/or made public by means of print, photographic print, microfilm, or in any other manner without the previous written consent of the Stichting Concilium, Nijmegen (Holland), T. & T. Clark Ltd., Edinburgh (Scotland) and The Seabury Press Inc., New York (USA).

October 1982
T. & T. Clark Ltd., 36 George Street, Edinburgh EH2 2LQ
ISBN: 0 567 30038 2

The Seabury Press, 815 Second Avenue, New York, NY 10017
ISBN: 0 8164 2389 X

Library of Congress Catalog Card No.: 81 85845
Printed in Scotland by William Blackwood & Sons Ltd., Edinburgh

Concilium: Monthly except July and August
Subscriptions 1982: UK and Rest of the World £27·00, postage and handling included; USA and Canada, all applications for subscriptions and enquiries about *Concilium* should be addressed to The Seabury Press, 815 Second Avenue, New York, NY 10017, USA.

CONTENTS

Editorial: The Right to Dissent
HANS KÜNG
JÜRGEN MOLTMANN ... vii

Part I
The Meaning of the Term

What does the 'Right to Dissent' mean in the Church?
PETER HUIZING and KNUT WALF ... 3

Part II
Dealing with Dissent in the Churches

The Catholic Church and Dissent
JAMES PROVOST ... 13

The Attitude of the Orthodox Church towards Dissent
KONSTANTIN VOICU ... 19

The Protestant Churches and Dissent
ALBERT STEIN ... 24

Part III
Dissent and Reaction in the History of the Church

Cyprian and Rome: The Controversy over Baptism
FRANCINE CARDMAN ... 33

Sect or Order? (Waldensians—Franciscans)
PAOLO RICCA ... 40

A Revolt of the Church against the Church? (Luther)
MARTIN BRECHT ... 47

The Dissent of Theology: The Modernist Crisis
GABRIEL DALY ... 53

Part IV
Biblical Norms

Prophets and Wise Men as Provokers of Dissent
  ROLAND E. MURPHY   61

Dealing with Dissenters in the New Testament Communities
  HERMANN-JOSEF VENETZ   67

Paul as a Witness to Dissent
  PAUL HOFFMANN   75

Part V
Clarifications

Confrontation as a Means of Communication in Theology, Church and Society
  JOSÉ MÍGUEZ BONINO   83

The Importance of Organised Opposition Groups and their Rights in the Church
  JUAN JOSÉ TAMAYO-ACOSTA   88

Part VI
Synthesis

The Rights and Limits of Dissent
  HERMANN HÄRING   95

Contributors   108

Editorial:
The Right to Dissent

THE RIGHT TO DISSENT: this subject has been constantly discussed in *Concilium* and considered in various contexts. In 1971 a volume on 'Contestation in the Church' was published. In 1973 the question whether parties are possible within the Church was considered, and volumes devoted to liberation theology and feminist theology have tackled the problem in their own way. It is clear that the life of the Church has included dissent at all periods of its history. It includes it today.

In 1973 the issue on Ecumenism began with the sentence: '*Concilium* is not a faction and does not wish to be a faction.' Nevertheless the affirmation of plurality in the Church was unequivocal. The opening sentence of this issue might run, '*Concilium* is not in love with dissent and does not seek to propagate it for its own sake.' But this journal does seek to ensure that in the Church today divergent voices and movements *find a hearing*. That much it owes to its name. It is no accident that the last contribution discusses the conciliar nature of the Church. A Church with a conciliar structure takes every contribution to discussion seriously. It is not afraid of cultural, geographical or social variety; rather, it places its trust in the honesty of all those who want to join it in thinking, talking and doing. Only that sort of Church could have the power to encourage reconciliation and liberation even while itself becoming the scene and mere reflection (reproducer) of social conflicts.

The structure and logic of this volume are easily recognised. The opening contributions are concerned with the clarification of terms and the compilation of an ecumenical *balance sheet*. Specific possibilities for coming to terms with dissent obviously reflect specific difficulties, but it is no solution to ignore dissent, to pretend it does not exist or simply to suppress it. Spotlights are next turned on figures and periods in the Church's history in which dissent was exercised as an accepted right, at least tolerated to the benefit of the Church, or to its detriment rejected or even the object of preventive repression. The damage done by intolerance is indisputable. It would be fatal if we were to fall back into outdated habits.

The *exegetical contributions* make two points. Dissent is a structural element in the history of Israel and the early Church, and for that very reason while we may discover tendencies and principles, there can be no general rules to determine its rights or its limits. The Gospel, we are reminded, is not letter but spirit made flesh in Jesus of Nazareth. It is therefore much more important to look for ecclesial forms and contexts in which dissent can be appropriately integrated, considered and made fruitful for the whole community.

The two *sociologically based contributions* can help us to make a sober assessment of dissent in the Church. Firstly, it is part of the life of any community which does not want to fossilise. Secondly, dissent is practised within our own Church—to its immense benefit—by entire groups in a responsible Christian way. They do not fragment the Church—quite the reverse.

The *last contribution* reviews the conclusions and develops them particularly in an ecumenical context. However great the need for the churches internally and mutually to take dissent seriously, this must never lead to a situation in which dissent becomes an ideology. What is needed rather is a profound trust in the Spirit of Christ to hold the balance between criticism and acceptance.

Häring says that dissent loses its rights when it refuses to be open to dialogue within the Church and explicitly forsakes the common basis of faith and discipleship. This conclusion may sound obvious, but *keeping the boundaries so wide* is all-important. Only in this way can the Church be preserved as a living organism which can tolerate dissent and find the strength to come to terms with it in itself and so to grow and mature.

HANS KÜNG
JÜRGEN MOLTMANN

PART I

The Meaning of the Term

Peter Huizing and Knut Walf

What does the 'Right to Dissent' mean in the Church?

MANY PEOPLE may be amazed to learn that there is a right to dissent in the Church. Nevertheless the evidence both from the past and from the current legal documents, both from legal theory and from law as it operates in the Church, is abundant and many-faceted. However, in the hierarchically structured organisation which is the Catholic Church there are something like differences in kind between the right to dissent enjoyed by the bishops and the right to dissent recognised as belonging to the laity. We shall look first at the position of the bishops.

1. THE RIGHT TO DISSENT WITHIN THE HIERARCHY

(a) The bishops' right of remonstration

Among the well-known and recognised writers on canon law (the so-called *auctores probati*) there has been, and continues to be down to the present, frequent discussion of what would happen if a universal Church regulation (a papal ruling) was resisted or ignored by those to whom it applied. Some of the most suggestive contributions to this topic were made by *Francisco Suarez* (d. 1619), who is frequently and gladly cited by later writers.

Suarez regards such a conflict as allowing for the possibility of what is known as 'supplication', not so much a right to dissent as a right to petition or entreaty, perhaps the right to gentle dissent. It is interesting, however, that Suarez justifies this right by the multiple nature of the Church and its local churches.[1] According to Suarez the supplication does not have the effect of postponing the application of the regulation, but in cases where application encounters great difficulty he regards the force of the law as suspended.

In particular the leaders of the local churches, that is the bishops, have the right, and even the duty, to be aware of the unease of those affected by the regulation and inform the pope of it. In this case the relevant literature talks not—like Suarez—of supplication but of the bishops' right to remonstration or objection *vis-à-vis* the Holy See. This is a completely accepted part of canon law, even if one which is little known today.

This episcopal right of remonstrance itself includes a suspensory effect. It was recognised in this broad sense explicitly and on several occasions in dealings with 'remonstrating' bishops by Pope *Alexander III* (1159-1181), who was a well-known canon lawyer (Rolando Bandinelli). As a result of its importance for the law of the Church in general the bishops' right of remonstrance was incorporated into the *decretals of Gregory IX* and is therefore part of the *Corpus Iuris Canonici*,[2] the official collection of laws which reflected the law of the Church until the CIC of 1917/18. However authoritative modern writers on canon law, such as Michiels, also stress that a remonstrance on the part of bishops against a papal law postpones its effect.[3]

As already mentioned, the authorities regard the legitimacy of the right of remonstrance as rooted in the multiplicity resulting from the development of local churches. Such considerations also appear in texts of the *Corpus Iuris Canonici*, for example in the *Liber Sextus of Boniface* VIII (c. 1 in VI⁰ 1, 2), that is, right at the beginning of this book. According to this a universal Church law cannot derogate from local church law or customs in so far as these are reasonable. Popes of later periods, especially those of the post-Tridentine centuries, attempted to curb the legal institution of the episcopal remonstrance, even Benedict XIV, who, as a canonist had given a very positive account of the legal powers of local churches. In this context it will be remembered that the Council of Trent had regarded bishops as *vicarii papae*. The great majority of canonists, however, even in these periods, consistently defended the right of episcopal remonstrance and tried to justify it, even after the coming into force of the CIC, which says nothing about it.

Naturally episcopally minded canonists of the eighteenth century took a particular interest in these issues. This may even explain why later generations of canonists devoted less attention to this subject and were less vigorous in their efforts to produce arguments based in ecclesiology. Nevertheless it must be recognised that, for example, the Josephinist canon lawyers in relation to this question showed a keen awareness of a venerable tradition which was fully justified. So, for example, Abbot *Martin Gerbert* regarded episcopal opposition to the pope as possible, and indeed as essential, when the bishops believed that the pope was issuing an instruction which did not contribute to the building up of the churches under their charge and was not in accordance with laws and properly established customs.[4] But these canon lawyers were not defending pure opposition by bishops to the pope. Dissent—they argued—made necessary a process for reaching agreement, for which there needed to be institutional provision in the Church. The conclusion drawn by the Josephinist inclined canonist *Paul Joseph von Riegger* was that in decisions on important questions of common interest the bishops should deliberate *and decide* with the pope. Other canonists of this period pointed out that the bishops were like brothers of the pope, not under-age sons. A further conclusion from this was that dissent, remonstrance, could not be the end of the road: logically these steps must be followed by consultation. Conversely, early consultation avoids a situation in which bishops too frequently resort to the (final) step of remonstrance. More will be said about this below.

It was not only the episcopally minded canonists of the eighteenth century who judged the legal institution of the remonstrance legitimate and held it to be indispensable. It was also mentioned by more than one canon lawyer even after the dogma of 1870. Particularly worthy of mention here is the German canonist *J. B. Haring*, a central theme of whose work is the defence of 'the episcopal right to present objections to the Holy See'.

It has already been noted that the *CIC of 1917/18* does not mention the bishops' right of remonstrance, and this is true also of the draft for a new CIC. On the other hand, the CIC does contain the basis for its legitimation. Haring, for example, argued that this could be attempted by the application of the CIC's doctrine of rescripts (cc. 36-62). In 1978 H. Müller rightly insisted that after the Second Vatican Council and its understanding of the Church there could no longer be any doubt that the right of episcopal remonstrance had a legitimate place in the legal system of the Catholic Church.

When the draft for a *Basic Law of the Church* (*Lex Ecclesiae Fundamentalis*, LEF), concedes the right of individual members of the Church, and even obliges them, to express their views to the bishops on matters affecting the welfare of the Church (LEF 12, §3), this applies with particular force to bishops in their relationship with the pope! It is regrettable, however, that this particular point is not explicitly made in those passages of the LEF which deal with the collaboration of the pope and the episcopal college.

It is also a matter of regret to find that the draft of the *new CIC* makes no legal provision at all for redress against inadequate or doubtful laws. This must be regarded as a real gap in the law, since allowance must be made in any legal system for the possibility of defective laws and dissent.

The right of bishops to object to papal decrees is, then, regarded by canonists of all periods as undeniable and indeed both obvious and necessary. This makes it all the more surprising that the Church's new law-code, which has as one of its aims to take account of and incorporate the conclusions of the Second Vatican Council, makes no mention of this fundamental episcopal right. Objection is as a rule necessary when there has been inadequate consultation in the preparation of a legal regulation. If therefore the legal machinery governing consultation between the pope and the bishops, between the leadership of the universal Church and the leadership of the local churches, were provided for more convincingly in the new law than hitherto, it might be possible to understand the absence of any explicit reference to the right to dissent. In fact, the *possibilities for consultation*, at least consultation on a broad and representative basis, are totally inadequate in the new law; indeed, *in comparison with the previous law they have been reduced*. For example, the new law of the Church (LEF and the new CIC) gives less prominence to the role of ecumenical councils, and yet the council is uniquely the symbol of a synodal and collegial structure in the Church, is the guarantee of consultation between pope and bishops.

As a canonist, one quite often has the impression that the general law of the Church created and promulgated by the pope formally allows no room, or too little room, for objections and the right to consultation, in order not to restrict the independence of the primacy. In fact, however, and, significantly, increasingly since the First Vatican Council, before particularly important decisions popes have taken a great deal of trouble to reach a consensus with the worldwide episcopate. Precisely this fact raises the question why there is no adequate provision for either objection or the attainment of consensus in canon law or institutional structures.

(b) Objections to Judicial Decisions

A final point which should be considered is the fact that Catholic canon law, even as late as the eighteenth and nineteenth centuries, was aware of, and formally recognised, the importance of judicial decisions for the development of law. The tendency today, after two codifications of Catholic canon law in a single century, to regard this legal system as a rigid code of (papal) statute law gives no indication of the original richness of the canonical tradition. Canon law always recognised and prized the creative function of judges in developing the law. Judicial decisions, however, can give rise to conflict with traditional law and its interpretation. Today in the Catholic Church dissenting judgments by an independent judge are rare and occur generally only in the highest (papal) courts, and then usually only in marriage cases. Judicial decisions which diverge from generally accepted interpretations, especially in the lower tribunals, are regarded as dangerous and objectionable signs of disruption: an obvious example is Rome's calling to order of the marriage tribunals in the Netherlands and the USA.

It is above all the local churches within the sphere of influence of Anglo-American law which find the rigidity of Catholic canon law alien, since they have come to value the flexibility and potential for development which case law gives to civil law. To *legal positivism*, which is what we are faced with in modern Catholic canon law, however, dissent is not only something abhorrent; it is simply inconceivable. On the other hand, a legal system without the formalised possibility of dissent inevitably decays and dies. The lawgiver must build on the experience and decisions of autonomous judges who, as it were, in confrontation with everyday life have to reach a balance between the acceptance and adaptation of existing law. If this possibility is denied to judges or—as in the Catholic Church—silently made taboo because all that is expected from them is a totally uncritical and compliant application of the letter of the law to actual cases, the lawgiver's decisions will for the most part fall into a void with no connection with life. (K.W.)

2. THE LAITY'S RIGHT TO DISSENT

Obedience and conscience. However strongly the virtues of obedience and submissiveness to lawful authority and its prescriptions have been emphasised in the Catholic Church and however much they have occasionally seemed to be treated as absolute—we need think only of 'the dead body which can be carried anywhere and treated in any fashion' or 'the stick in the hand of an old man which allows itself to be used wherever and for whatever purpose he wishes', with which Ignatius of Loyola compared his completely obedient sons[5]—nevertheless an absolute positivism of power and law has never been accepted theoretically in the Church. Even Ignatius set an absolute limit to obedience and the rights of authority: '. . . at least where it is clear . . . that no sin is involved.'[6] The person who has to decide in such a case whether sin is involved or not is clearly not the authority, but the subordinate. It is important to realise the full implication of that: a judgment by an authority on what someone has to do always depends in the last resort on the ethical and moral judgment of conscience of the person concerned. Where authority and rules are in conflict with individual conscience, the individual is obliged to oppose and to object, at least by not following the authority's instruction. This is the individual's inherent right.

No legal positivism. The sort of legal positivism which teaches that the existence and force of any law is rooted in 'the will of the lawgiver' has never been ultimately accepted even in the tradition of canon law. Even the medieval compilers of collections of laws such as Bishop Ivo of Chartres and the monk Gratian of Bologna were aware that ecclesiastical authority and ecclesiastical law can never have force, force of law, if they do not agree with *quod iure naturae et evangelio continetur*, in other words, if they do not agree with the principles contained in 'natural law' and 'divine law'. If ecclesiastical authority and ecclesiastical law come into conflict with these, the faithful have the duty and the right to protest against them and to oppose any such exercise of power and any such law.

Since ethical principles and the principles of Christian morality may be infringed not only by the deliberate actions of individuals, but also by social and ecclesiastical structures, opposition to authority and law does not always necessarily mean a deliberate rejection of particular people, in practice those who are members of the hierarchy. Particularly in periods of fundamental change in Church and society such as we are living through in the last quarter of this century, it is unavoidable that situations of conflict should arise between those responsible for the continued existence and unity of the community and those who are the intellectual and political promoters of such developments. In such a situation critics cannot be denied the right to publish, propagate and defend their view of things, and to do so, if necessary, in opposition to the existing order and existing authority, provided that they are convinced in conscience that the order and authority are objectively unjust obstacles to free development.

The fundamental rejection of legal positivism by the Church's law is perhaps shown most clearly by the fact that the whole tradition of canon law knows and recognises legal forms which legitimate the rejection of positive law on the basis of the principles of the law itself.

Acceptance of law. Although the formal validity of an ecclesiastical law does not depend on the agreement of the people or its acceptance of the law (*acceptatio*), the tradition of canon law generally assumes that when a law in practice cannot be implemented, is not observed and so remains a dead letter, such a law *in practice loses its validity* and ceases to exist as genuine law. The right of remonstrance enjoyed by the authority in the local church, which was mentioned above, rests on the possibility that difficulties may arise with the people if a particular new law is promulgated or particular decisions are taken by the leadership of the Church. In such a case the likely opposition of the people may be a sign that the law or the measure is inappropriate and in consequence the people's opposition must be regarded as legitimate. In such a case the authority concerned is obliged to rethink the planned introduction of the law or the planned ruling, taking into account the reasons or the causes underlying the opposition.

Custom versus law. Positive Church law sanctions the non-acceptance of a positive law or opposition to it in advance by recognising that in certain circumstances custom has a legal force which overrides statute (*consuetudo contra legem*). The precondition for this is that the custom is not immoral and has been regarded by the community in question as legally binding;[7] a term is stipulated for this recognition, forty years according to the 1917/18 code still formally in force and twenty years according to the draft for a new code. Even if an ecclesiastical law contains a clause prohibiting contrary customs in the future, such a custom acquires legal force when it has existed for a long period. The codex speaks in this context of a custom which has lasted for 100 years or from time immemorial (*consuetudo centenaria aut immemorabilis*). In other words, the law itself recognises that a custom maintained by the people in defiance of the law may acquire legal force and so deprive the law of its legal force. Both the current codex and the new draft maintain the principle that the custom which defies the law possesses no legal force unless it has been approved by the lawgiver, but this simply means that the custom must meet the above-mentioned criteria defined by the law in order not simply to exist in practice but also to have legal validity. It does not mean that the custom acquires legal force only through a particular formal legal enactment of the lawgiver. *Custom is a source of law not only formally but really distinct from statute*; it is therefore incontrovertibly a making of law by the community or the people and not by the lawgiver.

The right to participation. The catalogue of basic rights and duties of all the faithful in the draft of the *Lex Ecclesiae Fundamentalis* includes the right of participation. The faithful have the right to make their needs, especially in spiritual matters, and their wishes known to the ecclesiastical authorities, and according to their knowledge, their competence and their position they have the right, and occasionally even the duty 'to express to their ordained pastors their views on matters which affect the welfare of the Church and, after taking due account of the common good and personal dignity, to inform the faithful of them'.[8] A right to participation naturally also exists in *synodal structures*, from the synod of bishops to diocesan councils of priests and pastoral councils and parish councils. Even though the texts cited from the *Lex Ecclesiae Fundamentalis* contain some unjuridical moralising clauses, and although the synodal right of participation is timidly limited to being 'purely consultative'—a paternalism unknown to the apostolic Council of Jerusalem and the medieval councils—it is impossible to give serious recognition to a right of participation if it does not include the right to express a divergent opinion and thus the right to dissent. Participation designed merely to confirm the views of authority is valueless. If a pope does not take part in the discussion at an episcopal synod for fear of restricting the freedom of his fellow bishops to express their opinions, the freedom to express one's opinion cannot have been worth very much in the first place. A leadership which cannot tolerate a 'loyal opposition' is—particularly in the Church and in the churches—more of a threat than a support to the unity and cohesiveness of the Church.

Fraternal correction. The final point which needs to be dealt with in this connection is 'fraternal correction' (*correctio fraterna*). The most famous New Testament example of this is *Paul's public protest against Peter* in Antioch when Peter, from fear of the Jewish Christians in James's circle, began to draw back from eating with Gentile Christians. By this action he brought the Gentile Christians into a situation in which they were obliged to separate themselves from the community or observe the Jewish dietary laws and perhaps even the whole Jewish law (Gal. 2.11-14). Naturally it would be wrong to imagine that the community at Antioch experienced this as a protest by Bishop Paul against Pope Peter, but it must have impressed the community that such a distinguished member of the community as Paul should protest so openly and so vigorously against the man with the highest standing among the apostles of Jesus. At any rate the scene was remembered and was preserved in the Church's tradition as paradigmatic.

Medieval scholasticism in its own day had a developed doctrine of fraternal correction based on the principle that Christians, as brothers and sisters, are responsible for each other and therefore also obliged, when necessary and possible, to warn and guard one another from harm and error. This duty and the corresponding right is enjoyed by all Christians, though naturally within the bounds of their actual capabilities. This accordingly applies to superiors in relation to their subordinates, to equals among each other and to subordinates in relation to their superiors. In the middle ages this right was exercised in relation to popes by princes or by people of great personal standing such as St Bernard, and the cardinals regarded it as one of the duties of their office to correct the pope where necessary.

Service to the community. Criticism, opposition and, where necessary, protest from the Church community against a wrong use of power or against the maintenance of wrong structures and norms has always been regarded by the Church's tradition as possible, though naturally under certain conditions. It is a right enjoyed by members of the Church, and can in some circumstances become a positive Christian duty. In order to be truly Christian and truly of the Church the right to dissent must naturally be founded on respect for lawful authority and the order of law, and finally on service to the community, since it exists for the sake of good authority and good law.[9] (P.H.).

Translated by Francis McDonagh

Notes

1. Richard Potz *Die Geltung kirchenrechtlicher Normen* (Vienna 1978) p. 114. See *ibid*. p. 239ff. Other writing on the subject: Johann Haring 'Das bischöfliche Vorstellungsrecht gegenüber dem Apostolischen Stuhle' *AkathKR* 91 (1911) 111ff.; Hubert Müller *Das Gesetz in der Kirche 'zwischen' amtlichem Anspruch und konkretem Vollzug, Eichstätter Hochschulreden*, vol. 13 (Munich 1978).

2. c. 5 X 1, 3 and c. 6 X 1, 5.

3. Gommarus Michiels *Normae Generales Iuris Canonici* (Parisiis-Tornaci-Romae, 2a ed. 1949) pp. 198f.: 'Communissima etiam est Auctorum doctrina, legem pontificiam, contra quam de facta instituta fuerit remonstratio ista, interim, idest, usquedum obtentum fuerit contrarium Sedis Apostolicae responsum, non esse exsequendam aut urgendam.'

4. Knut Walf *Das bischöfliche Amt in der Sicht josephinischer Kirchenrechtler* (Cologne and Vienna 1975) p. 88.

5. *Constitutions*, 547. Translated from the Dutch version, Manuscriptum Berchmanium (Nijmegen 1966-67) p. 151.

6. *Ibid*.

7. Such a community must also passively be a subject of law, i.e., it must be large and permanent enough for laws to be made for it.

8. c. 12, § 3 LEF (1976).

9. Peter Huizing 'The Church and Contestation' in *Concilium* 68 (1971) at p. 96.

PART II

Dealing with Dissent in the Churches

James Provost

The Catholic Church and Dissent

'*CATHOLIC*' implies breadth of vision and inclusiveness, an openness to all cultures and peoples. One of the characteristics of the Catholic Church is *diversity*, expressed in the variety of rites in its communion, schools of thought and prayer, and in its many diverse peoples and cultures.

'*Dissent*', on the other hand, implies going beyond the limits of diversity. It is the opposite of consent. It may relate to an entire system of belief, or be a *refusal to consent* to some truth, belief or practice, or non-conformity to the accepted way of doing things.

Within the Catholic Church the right to dissent is guaranteed to those involved in elections, consultative processes, or whose consent may be required by law. Such dissent is not the object of this study. Rather, we will explore how the Roman Catholic Church deals with those who refuse consent to significant teachings on *faith and morals*, or who refuse consent to accepted ways of doing things in the church. Our study will address defining consent, church officials and the limits of dissent, theologians and dissent, rights and responsibilities of believers, and some contemporary tensions.

1. DEFINING CONSENT

(*a*) Types of dissent

In our context dissent can be from the Gospel, from the teaching of the Church, or on practical issues where dissent is from decisions of Church authorities.

Legal definitions of dissent are given in the Church's code of law.[1] An *apostate* is defined as one who totally rejects the Christian faith. A *heretic* is one who retains the Christian name but pertinaciously denies or doubts some of the truths to be believed by divine and catholic faith. A *schismatic* is one who dissents by refusing to submit to the pope or to be in communion with members of the Church subject to him. These legal categories apply to those who dissent from the Gospel and from the teaching of the Church. Their application to dissent on practical issues is one of the debated areas in Catholic life.

(*b*) Processes of definition

The process of defining dissent in practical cases is supposed to have *two components* in the Catholic Church. One component determines the criteria upon which a judgment can be made to classify a position as dissent; this is a function of *magisterium* or *teaching authority*. The other component applies these criteria to practical cases; this is a function of *pastoral authority*, the hierarchy of jurisdiction.

Until recent times these two elements were held in *creative tension*. The interaction of saints, scholars and councils clarified the criteria of orthodoxy and orthopraxis. The hierarchy of pope and diocesan bishops charged with pastoral government applied the criteria to local situations. In the nineteenth century, however, the two elements were fused into the work of the *same persons*. A theory has developed to subject the teaching authority (*magisterium*) to pastoral rules in the Church (jurisdiction).[2] This has clouded the issue of dissent for Roman Catholics. *Dissent in matters of faith becomes a question of discipline, while dissent in matters of discipline can be treated as a question of faith.*

(c) Limits

The system does recognise some limits, however, and these must be respected to avoid judging a position to be in dissent when actually it pertains to the legitimate diversity of the Catholic *communion*. Such limits are set by the *diversity of rites*, schools of thought, and process of change in the Church. Ritual churches 'sui iuris', or the various rites of the Church, are more than diverse liturgical practices. Vatican II characterised them as also distinguishable on the basis of government and discipline, theological patrimony, and spiritual tradition.[3] Rites are in communion, not dissent, even though they differ one from another.

Schools of thought are recognised as legitimately diverse within the Catholic community. A standard caution at the councils has been to avoid resolving questions which are legitimately debated among the *schools*. Similarly, schools of piety, of apostolic action, and of religious life exist side by side within the communion of Catholicism and are not considered in dissent.

There are mechanisms for change within the Catholic system in regard to both discipline and teaching. When differences occur as a result of these mechanisms, they are not considered dissent but *legitimate diversity*. For example, discipline changes through custom, dispensation, and particular law. In doctrinal questions the core of truth is distinguished from changeable elements in its expression; distinctions are made between Tradition and traditions, between the object of faith and its formulation; a hierarchy has been officially recognised among the various truths to be held.[4]

2. CHURCH OFFICIALS AND LIMITS OF DISSENT

The purpose for Church office is to *foster the communion* of the Christian faithful and to promote the mission of the Church. In so far as dissent touches this communion or mission it is of concern to Church officials. Canon law expresses this when it says that the judgment about such matters is the responsibility of bishops (CIC 1326), and in a particular way of the Holy See (CIC 1324). Three aspects of this concern will be discussed: the levels of responsibility; procedures to fulfil this responsibility; and responses employed by Church officials.

(a) Levels of responsibility

The primary responsibility for addressing dissent belongs to the *local bishop*. While he exercises this individually, traditionally the bishops of a region have considered dissent in provincial councils. These legal structures remain today (CIC 290), even if they are seldom used.

Conferences of bishops developed since Vatican II are to be concerned for doctrine and discipline, so the question of dissent could appropriately be considered by these groups. However, their decisions are generally not binding nor do they have the provincial council's authority to pass judgment. Conferences have been encouraged to establish *committees on doctrine*; their function is to engage in dialogue and to keep the Apostolic See informed, rather than to resolve questions of dissent locally.[5]

Within the present legal framework of the Catholic Church and in keeping with the decisions of Vatican II, the *Apostolic See* exercises a special role in questions of dissent. An ancient expression of the Petrine ministry has been to serve as court of last resort in disputes, including dissent over teaching or discipline. Today the Apostolic See continues that function not only in receiving appeals but also by initiating investigations and exercising general supervision through the primacy of jurisdiction. It can order compliance with its decisions through legal enactments such as constitutions and decrees (CIC 1324), and can order dissenters to conform by using administrative precepts.

In addition to the pope's specific responsibilities in fulfilling the Petrine office, a formal structure has existed at the Apostolic See since the sixteenth century to address questions of dissent. Founded in 1542 by Paul III, the *Sacred Congregation of the Universal Inquisition* was the first of the modern dicasteries or bureaus which form the Roman Curia. Previously, *ad hoc* commissions of cardinals had addressed issues brought to the papal court. Now a standing commission was established whose powers, extended by Pius IV, enabled it to act on dissent in any form, by any member of the Church, of whatever rank.[6]

The institutionalisation of concern over dissent altered the Holy See's approach from pastoral to *bureaucratic*. A professional staff and specialised procedures were developed. The reforms of 1908 when the congregation became known as the *Holy Office*, and of 1965 when it became the *Doctrinal Congregation*, continued this approach. The major change has been to publicise its procedures, not to change their fundamentally inquisitorial nature.

(b) **Procedures**

Judicial procedures exist for assessing the acceptability of dissent in particular cases. Councils sit in judgment; bishops are judges of faith and discipline in their dioceses. One accused of heresy or even suspect of it can be brought to trial through the criminal procedures of the code (CIC 1933-1959).

Judicial procedures with their safeguards and time delays are rarely used today. Through the *combination of magisterium and jurisdiction into one office* and the general subordination of *magisterium* to jurisdiction in practice, bishops acting alone and the Apostolic See itself generally use *administrative procedures*. This is especially true when dissenters are pastors, teachers in Catholic institutions, or others subject to the administrative control of Church officers.

The Doctrinal Congregation has its own special procedures which it characterises as a *'process for truth'* rather than a criminal procedure. It lacks many of the safeguards guaranteed an accused person under criminal procedure in canon law, as do procedures bishops are to follow in the prior censorship of books.[7]

(c) **Responses**

When faced with dissent in the Church, officials must decide whether to admit it or to attempt to end it. Admitting dissent can take the form of dissimulation, pretending not to know about the dissent in order to avoid taking any action. Or, more direct *toleration* of dissent can be adopted.

Toleration has a mixed history in the Catholic Church, much of it a factor of the times and of Church-State relations. In the light of principles adopted at Vatican II—especially on religious liberty, the pilgrim nature of the people of God, and legitimate pluralism in theology—toleration has been proposed as a *formal principle* for the internal constitution of the Church.[8] In fact, toleration is the general response to dissent in the Catholic Church today, so much so that sociologically the Church has been compared to a 'lazy monopoly'.[9]

There are *limits to toleration*. It does not apply when the existence of the Church itself or the faith of any member is endangered. At the 1974 Synod of Bishops a proposal was made to explore the norms for dissent within the Church, and at least one bishop has suggested norms which should be observed in practice if dissent is to be tolerated.[10]

If Church officials decide not to tolerate dissent there are various *penal remedies* in the law which attempt to end dissent and obtain the desired consent (CIC 2214-2313). Some of these are 'medicinal', directly intended to lead the dissenter to a change of heart. Other penalties are 'vindictive', or as the revised Code proposes to call them, 'expiatory'. Even if the dissenter changes his mind they are applied to impress all with the seriousness of the dissent.

Various *administrative measures* are available to bishops, the Doctrinal Congregation, and other officials of the Holy See. These range from a warning or even public condemnation, to prohibition of writing or teaching.

There are limits to the remedies Church officials can apply to dissenters. They themselves are bound to the standards of revelation, respect for the dignity and rights of persons, and the reformability of ordinary, fallible teaching. In addition, the role of theologians and the rights and responsibilities of all believers temper the otherwise dominant role of the hierarchy.

3. THEOLOGIANS AND DISSENT

The issue of dissent by theologians has been raised by various events before and after Vatican II. Several attempts have been made to suggest structures for dissent, providing for a sort of 'loyal opposition' by theologians.

The International Theological Commission suggested some *principles for dialogue* between theologians and the ecclesiastical *magisterium*. The German Episcopal Conference adopted rather complex procedures for settling grievances in matters relating to doctrine.[11] Neither approach has found widespread acceptance. A joint committee of the canon law and theological societies in the United States is attempting to develop norms for dialogue and resolution of disputes between theologians and the ecclesiastical *magisterium* in that country.[12]

As Yves Congar recently pointed out, the issue is broader than the intramural concern of Catholics.[13] It touches the core of the *ecumenical imperative* facing the churches today. Recognising legitimate theological dissent is not beyond the traditions of the Catholic Church, but it is hindered by the overly juridical approach to *magisterium* and the role of theologians which has marked the Catholic communion in recent times.

4. RIGHTS AND RESPONSIBILITIES OF BELIEVERS

Ultimately the communion and mission of the Church are the work of the Spirit. *Charisms*, distributed widely according to Vatican II and without respect for rank or status, give rise to rights and obligations within the Church and in the world for their use.[14] A charism may lead one prophetically to dissent. Church officials must not extinguish the spirit but moderate the exercise of charisms for the good of all.

The church must incarnate the Gospel in diverse cultures. Dissent can easily arise when there are attempts to impose a culturally conditioned manner of expressing the Gospel as the standard for other *cultures*. The overextension of the Latin Rite from its cultural roots cannot help but occasion such dissent in practice.

Dissent among believers also arises when the official practices and directives of the Church fail to take into account legitimate diversity of opinion. There is widespread dissent in practice from moral teachings of modern popes, ranging from sexual ethics to social justice. To what extent does this dissent arise from sin, a turning from the Gospel? To what extent is it genuine dissent in matters rightfully left to private decision? There has been little effort to respond to such questions officially.

5. SOME CONTEMPORARY TENSIONS

Dissent is a more *widespread phenomenon* in the Catholic Church today than at any time in the preceding century. Dissent in practice exists in regard to moral teaching on sexual ethics, social justice, and issues of war and peace. Practical dissent, in terms of non-compliance, exists in regard to liturgical discipline, the exercise of official functions, and procedures to be observed in various Church activities. This dissent comes from bishops, pastors, theologians, individuals, organised groups. At the same time, the principles for dealing with dissent are undergoing transition. This leads to inconsistent official practice. At times, norms in pre-conciliar laws are invoked; at other times, a more rigid interpretation is applied to post-conciliar legislation; at still other times, dissimulation or tolerance is practised on the same issues.

What appears needed is a *consensus about the legitimacy of dissent* and the limits beyond which dissent is unacceptable. Some suggestions have been made for criteria of such limits, but little progress can be observed towards developing effective procedures to implement this criteria. Episcopal conferences were viewed by Vatican II as key structures to make such applications, but their role is being downplayed in the revision of the code and marginalised by current practices of the Roman Curia.

Whether the situation can be remedied will depend on the honesty with which the current situation is addressed, the flexibility with which solutions are sought, and the integrity of all concerned for the Christian commitment that continues to make Catholics one communion.

Notes

1. *Codex Iuris Canonici* [CIC] canon 1325, § 2.
2. J. Boyle 'The Ordinary Magisterium: Towards a History of the Concept' *Heythrop Journal* 20 (1979) 380-398 and 21 (1980) 14-29.
3. *Orientalium Ecclesiarum* nos. 2 and 3.
4. *Unitatis redintegratio* no. 11.
5. S. Cong. pro Doct. Fidei, Letter to Presidents of Episcopal Conferences, 24 July 1966, *Nuntius* 1 (1967) 15-16.
6. R. Miller *The Congregation for the Doctrine of the Faith* (Canon Law Studies 484) (Washington 1975).
7. S. Cong. pro Doct. Fidei *Ratio agendi* (15 January 1971) *A.A.S.* 63 (1971) 234-236; *Ecclesiae pastorum* [on censorship of books] (19 March 1975) *A.A.S.* 67 (1975) 281-284.

8. J. Brinkmann *Toleranz in der Kirche* (Paderborn 1980).
9. J. Seidler 'Priest Resignations in a Lazy Monopoly' *American Sociological Review* 44 (1979) 763-783.
10. J. Quinn 'Norms for Church Dissent' [1974 Synod] *Origins* 4/20 (1974) 319-320; J. Arzube 'Criteria for Dissent in the Church' *Origins* 7/47 (1978) 748-750.
11. Int. Theo. Comm. 'Theses on the Relationship Between the Ecclesiastical Magisterium and Theology' 6 June 1976; 'Beschluss der Deut. Bischofkonferenz vom 21 September 1972 zur Regelung eines Lehrbeanstandungsverfahrens' *Arch. f. kath. Kirchenr.* 141 (1972) 524-530.
12. *Cooperation Between Theologians and Ecclesiastical Magisterium* ed. L. O'Donovan (Washington 1982).
13. Y. Congar *Diversités et Communion* (Paris 1982).
14. *Apostolicam actuositatem* no. 3.

Konstantin Voicu

The Attitude of the Orthodox Church towards Dissent

1. THE CONCERN TO PRESERVE THE TRUTH IN DIALOGUE

(a) **The care for one another in charity**

TO UNDERSTAND the attitude of the Orthodox Church towards the matter of dissent correctly one has to start with the fact that the Church has always been concerned about preserving its unity in the orthodox faith. The best analogy for the reality of the Church was given us by St Paul when he described the Church as a 'body', the *body of Christ*. This analogy implies at the same time the diversity of the members and the unity of the function. In 1 Cor. 12 St Paul elaborates this analogy and points to the organic interrelationship which prevails in the very constitution of the body which implies: 'that there may not be disagreements inside the body but that each part may be equally concerned for all the others' (*1 Cor.* 12:25). Significantly the Apostle devotes the next chapter of his Epistle to love and its gifts as if he wanted to point out that only this virtue which 'has no limit' can ensure the unity of the body, and therefore of the Church.

From the *Acts of the Apostles* we learn that the normal state of the Church is one of *unity*: 'They were all gathered together in one room' (*Acts* 2:1), and: 'The faithful all lived together and owned everything in common' (*Acts* 2:44).

The *faith* of the Church is a treasure held in common ('to find encouragement among you from our common faith', *Rom.* 1:12). It is as such that the Synods explain and explore it, again and again. The ecumenical Synods of the Church are the most relevant expression of its universality.

(b) **The Synods**

These Synods were convened when the common faith was threatened, particularly by heresy. They were meant to have a new look at this faith and to express it in a new and fresh way at a time when the Eastern Church had to deal with a number of heresies, particularly during the first ten centuries of Christianity. (In the West we usually talk about 'Councils', particularly when referring to General or Oecumenical Councils of the whole Church, but 'Synod' in the West most often has a geographically or thematically restricted connotation. According to the non-Roman Catholic Churches the last Oecumenical Council was that of Nicea in 787. The reader should read the following in the light of this clarification. *Trs*.) At the time of the Oecumenical Councils most heretics were members of the hierarchy, and very often *bishops*. This was the period in history when many truths contained in the faith of the Apostles required clarification. And one can take it for granted that a lot of heresies simply sprang from the need to have some convincing elucidation of these truths. Some of those who attempted this were deemed to be heretics in their exploration of the mysteries of the revelation: for instance, Arius.[1]

In such situations the Church has always opted for *dialogue*, as, for instance, between the simple priest Arius and Bishop Alexander, or among the bishops present at the Synod. Now, dialogue is essentially the opposite of one-sidedness. And this is precisely what heresy is about: the trend towards one-sidedness. The fact that the Synods accepted dialogue as the right way to proceed should make it clear that there is not only one facet to truth, that it has a paradoxical streak to it, that it is a union of opposites which are not mutually exclusive.

And so it was that the Church could learn that God is one and *yet* exists in three persons; that, on the one hand, the Son of God is not subject to change and *yet* can lower himself to assume common humanity and the death on the cross; that the divine as such cannot be directly shared and that, *all the same*, God can endow mankind with his own uncreated qualities; that in the Church the hierarchy has to co-exist with the community of their fellow-members in every sense of the word; and that the salvation of mankind cannot be achieved without *both* God's grace and man's concern for the whole human community.[2]

(c) The condemnation of heresy

If the other party to the dialogue maintained a one-track-minded approach then the Church saw itself compelled to condemn this lack of flexibility because it is bound to protect its unity, as well as the orthodoxy and mystery of its faith. In its rulings, its creeds and dogmas the purpose of the Church was not to put an end to the dialogue which would have already started before the Council took place and was, indeed, carried on during the Council. Moreover, the dialogue could always be taken up again as long as the new ideas and interpretations did not impair the essence of the faith, 'a treasure, inherited from Christ, which has to be preserved intact'.[3]

The classic example of such a doctrinal definition is the dogmatic statement of the Council of Chalcedon (A.D. 451) which defined the oneness of Christ's person in two natures as follows: He is 'One and the same Christ, Son, Lord, only-begotten, recognised as having two natures, which are neither mixed, nor changed, nor divided, nor separated'.

The dissent that leads to heresy, the rejection of communication through genuine dialogue, has its roots in *egoism*. And egoism means the obstinacy of one-track-mindedness, separation, divisiveness, the negation of love, and reducing life's potential to a lower level. It is essentially the contradiction of love which implies sincerity and the openness to continuous growth.

2. THE WAYS IN WHICH LEGITIMATE DISSENT CAN BE EXPRESSED

(a) The Believing People

The course of history has shown that the Orthodox Church knew of another form of protest or dissent than that of heresy.

It was aimed at the preservation of the Church's unity and the integrity of the faith. When necessary it was *the Christian believers* who defended this integrity against some Church leaders or the leadership of the Church as a whole.

(i) *Against heterodoxy and erroneous compromises*

For instance, the first to oppose Arius were his own audience, the common faithful. Another well-known example is the opposition of the faithful of Constantinople to the heretical teaching of Nestorius concerning the Mother of God. The people loudly voiced their desire to maintain 'the accustomed orthodox teaching'.[4] But the most striking illustration of the people's opposition to heretical Church authorities can be seen during the iconoclastic controversy.

As the Church authorities shared the opinion of the iconoclastic emperor and in the Synods looked for theological objections to the veneration of images, the people rose against the new heresy. This opposition was often expressed in violent ways.

One might also mention the position of the Orthodox people of Constantinople against the Church authorities when they wanted to enforce the conclusions reached at the Reunion Council of Florence (1438-45).

The faithful of the Ukraine resisted the Orthodox authorities who had subscribed to union with Rome in the sixteenth century.

In the eighteenth century the Orthodox Rumanians from Transylvania waged the same battle as in various ways they opposed the union with Rome which had been brought about by Bishop *Atanasie Anghel*.

In general Orthodox faithful and their clergy are subject to the bishop who is their ecclesiastical superior. They have to confess the same faith as he. But this obligation ceases as soon as this bishop no longer shares this Orthodox faith. Then *the people are obliged to oppose his false doctrine*.

Canons 1 and 2 of the Council of Constantinople show that the faithful are obliged to distance themselves from a bishop who spreads heretical doctrines. In such a situation they may not be punished but must be treated like those who proclaim their obedience to the bishop in ordinary circumstances.

On the contrary, these people must be admired for having opposed a *pseudo-bishop*. The people have then prevented a schism instead of starting one, and as a community they have separated themselves from heretics.[5]

(ii) *Acceptance ('Reception') of conciliar decisions*

In the Orthodox Church the faithful's right to dissent also holds good in the matter of conciliar decisions.

This process of a Council becoming accepted is slow and long, and is a burden which is *carried by the laity*. All Councils, considered by the Church leaders to be ecumenical, have to be accepted and recognised as such by the whole people of God. This recognition has in fact taken place in the case of some Councils, but not in the case of others. We all know that a number of Councils have been described as 'ecumenical'. But *only seven* of them have been accepted as such by all the faithful. And as it happened, it is evident that the line taken by the people of God in such cases proved totally justified.[6]

In the light of the position of the people of God this long process can be seen as a 'constitutive element' of the Church, without which 'the Church as such cannot exist and has no realistic meaning'.[7]

The 1848 Encyclical of the Orthodox Patriarchs states that 'the body of the Church, and that means the people of God' preserves and defends the faith.[8] So one may well come to the conclusion that in the cases mentioned above the laity have the right to dissent. This means that it is not merely a concession by the hierarchy. It is a constitutive element of the Church as such.

(b) The Monks

The opposition of layfolk to a hierarchy often inclined to unacceptable compromises was frequently led by the monks. And here we can again refer to the iconoclast controversy.

The monks maintained their resistance also after the 7th Ecumenical Council when the Church authorities were prepared to make concessions to the iconoclasts. Thus the Patriarchs of Constantinople Tarasius (784-806) and Methodius (843-847) allowed iconoclasts to stand as candidates for episcopal election. In the same way Tarasius and Nicephorus II (806-815) sanctioned Constantine VI's second marriage.[9] Of these prominent monks I only wish to refer to *Theodore of Studios* and *Nicephorus the Confessor*.

The part the monks played in defence of the faith is the reason why, at some time, it became customary to choose bishops from among the monks. And that is why Byzantine liturgical life bears the stamp of monasticism.[10]

Mention has already been made of the Orthodox *Rumanians* from Transylvania who in the eighteenth century were opposed to the concessions made by Bishop Atanasie Anghel and many of his clergy with regard to reunion with Rome.

In 1744 the monk *Visarion Sarai* stirred up the people to resist the re-united clergy and to support the institutions of the Orthodox Church.[11] At the same time another monk started a real ecclesiastical revolt against reunion with Rome.[12]

(c) The National Churches

Another form of dissent obtains in the Orthodox Church, namely, the tension which exists between the Orthodox national Churches and the Patriarchate of Constantinople, as well as heads of the Greek churches from the patriarchates of the East. Such dissent was precipitated by the control which Constantinople used to exercise over the various churches. So this opposition broke out when the *autonomy* of one or other church was rejected.

This form of dissent was frequently expressed in a dramatic way as, for instance, when in 1892 the people of Antioch were unable to make *their election of an Arab* as Patriarch prevail. When the Patriarch chosen in his stead came to the cathedral for his installation he found himself in an empty church.[13] The *Bulgarian schism* broke out when in 1872 the Patriarchate of Constantinople refused to recognise the autonomy of the Bulgarian Orthodox Church. This crisis was not solved until 1945 when this autonomy was accepted.[14]

3. THE CONCILIAR STRUCTURE OF THE ORTHODOX CHURCH

What has been said so far leads to the following conclusion: the history of the Orthodox Church shows that *dissent is legitimate*. Yet, the life of this Church is not characterised by dissent as such but rather by the preoccupation to maintain the dialogue. This preoccupation with dialogue stems from the conciliar structure of the Orthodox Church and from the conviction that its true Head is Jesus Christ in the Holy Spirit.

The relationship between hierarchy and people of God reveals itself in the most diverse ways as an expression of the dialogic structure. The starting-point of this dialogue lies in the way the priest and the laity respond to each other in the *liturgy*.

In this dialogue 'the priest proposes a way of confessing the faith and the people respond to it by accepting this'.[15]

This same dialogue marks the relationship between a bishop and the clergy and faithful in his diocese, and that of the bishops, gathered in council, with the other members of the Church.

This is why the direct opposition of the faithful to a parish priest or bishop only occurs in exceptional cases, that is to say, when the unity of the Church and the orthodoxy of the faith are threatened.

Translated by Theo Westow

Notes

1. A. Schmemann *The Historical Road of Eastern Christianity* (Chicago 1966) p. 75.
2. D. Stăniloae 'The Second Ecumenical Council and its importance for Christian Unity' in *Rumanian Orthodox Church News* 11 No. 1 (1981) 11.
3. Metropolitan E. Timiadis 'Reception, Consensus and Unity' in *The Greek Theological Review* 26 No. 1-2 (1981) 50-51.
4. J. D. Mansi *Sacrorum Conciliorum nova et amplissima collectio* IV col. 1105.
5. L. Stan *Mirenii în Biserica. Studiu canonic-istoric* (Sibiu 1939) pp. 101-102.
6. L. Stan 'Despre recepția de către Biserică a hotăririlor sinoadelor ecumenice' in *Studii Teologice* 27 No. 7-8 (1965) 399; J. Meyendorff 'What is an ecumenical council?' in *St Vladimir's Theological Quarterly* No. 17 (1973) 266; Metropolitan E. Timiadis *ibid.* 57.
7. L. Stan 'Poziția laicilor în Biserica Ortodoxă' in *Studii Teologice* 20 No. 3-4 (1968) 197.
8. T. M. Popescu 'Enciclica Patriarhilor ortodocsi de la 1848, trad în limba română', in *Biserica Ortodoxă Română* LIII 11-12 (1935) 676.
9. J. Meyendorff *Byzantine Theology Historical Trends and Doctrinal Themes* (New York 1974) p. 55.
10. *Ibid. The Orthodox Church. Its Past and its Role in the World Today* (London 1962) p. 78.
11. M. Răcurariu *Istoria Bisericii Ortodoxe Romane* II (Editura Institutului Biblic si de Misiune al Bisericii Ortodoxe Romane, Bucharest 1981) p. 384.
12. *Ibid.* p. 394.
13. S. Gholam 'Evolution et originalité de l'Eglise locale d'Antioche' in *Eglise locale et Eglise universelle* (Geneva 1981) p. 64.
14. T. Sabev 'Evolution et originalité de l'Eglise de Bulgarie' in *Eglise locale et Eglise universelle* p. 113.
15. D. Stăniloae 'Autoritatea Bisericii' in *Studii Teologice* 16 No. 3-4 (1964) 205.

Albert Stein

The Protestant Churches and Dissent

1. THE CONTENT OF THE CHURCH'S LAWS

THE WAY in which the Protestant Church deals with the dissent at the centre of its being in the continuous debate for the truth of the Gospel could, without too much difficulty, be made clear by giving a fairly detailed description of the large number of theological disputes and discussions about Church politics that have taken place at this level in recent years. Unfortunately, this would go far beyond the scope of an article in this journal. It would also involve a serious risk, in that it might appear to be tinged with the views either for or against one side of an author who is not able to be completely impartial in this controversial matter. This would mean that the article would lose its power to convince. For these reasons, I have preferred to take an analysis of the content of the Church's laws in this respect as my point of departure.

Both within the Church and outside it, one of the functions of legal norms is to help to give direction to decisions regarding forms of law in any contemporary conflict of interests. Apart from the cases in which they are practically applied at a later stage, they also point to the ideas held by those who devise them and determine the cause and the nature of future debates about legal matters within the Church and the possible ways of resolving these discussions.[1] If we do not become involved in dissent, we shall not need any formal laws to deal with such a situation of conflict. If we do not expect dissent in the future, we shall have no particular need to legislate and to take precautionary measures against it. If, on the other hand, we look forward in the Church to probable dissent in the future or are at least prepared to take this into account, we shall take preventive measures of a suitable kind in our Church laws. These measures will, moreover, not be taken exclusively in an 'emergency' as instruments for settling or suppressing conflicts. They will also provide the critical reviewer with a means of judging how a particular Church dealt with or intended to deal with its internal dissensions at a particular time.

With this in mind, a number of major points of view taken from the ecclesiastical law of the Protestant Churches in Germany and Austria will be presented and discussed in what follows in this article. It is not only because of their different theological perspectives and their individual Church politics that these Churches are particularly prone to inner contradictions—it is also because their different Church orders, which are for the most part based on various State or State-Church forms of law, provide a great deal of material for highly relevant remarks.

2. THE PARISH CLERGY AND POLITICAL CONFLICT

Dissent can begin with those who hold office in the Church and have the task of proclaiming the good news. In other words, it can begin with the clergy. It can also begin with the laity as official members of Church bodies at various levels and with simple lay people in the everyday sense of the word who belong to the people of God and to parish and other communities, but have no particular function to carry out within the Church as such. The law of the Protestant Churches takes the possibility of dissent into account in all three cases and has measures available that can be used to overcome that dissent. In what follows, I shall deal only with the first case, that of the clergy, because it is the most important and because it provides the most vivid example.

(a) An Analysis of the Situation

There is always a danger that the parish pastor[2] will, in the way in which he speaks and behaves not only in his public capacity, but also in his private life, contradict rather than fulfil the expectations that others have of him. These expectations are, after all, often different in the case of the Church authorities, his fellow-clergy, both those who are close to him and those who belong to a wider circle, influential members of his own parish community and people in a position of trust in the Church. He cannot possibly satisfy the expectations of all these groups of people in any way equally. On the other hand, however, he will inevitably be motivated, because of his theological training, to present his own views in an effective way to everyone in his community.

In the early years of his ministry particularly, he will, because of this, often find himself in a situation of conflict. The fact that he encounters contradiction and that he appears to others to be man who contradicts will not usually hold him back. Indeed, it may even seem to him to be a sign that he is carrying out his duty conscientiously. It has been said with good reason that the pastor who has not broken a pane of glass at least once in twenty years of his ministry certainly owes his parish something!

(b) Rules for the Pastor's Political Activity

It is hardly surprising that the detailed Church regulations and laws regarding the duties of the parish clergy[3] are quite precise in what they stipulate here. Their unmistakeable and primary aim is to prevent the possibility—which is regarded as a serious danger—that the parish clergy may become so active in fulfilling their political rights as citizens that they will be seen by members of their Christian communities whose political allegiance is different as political opponents rather than as pastors who can be trusted and are committed to care for them.

The prohibition against playing an active part in the work of political parties may help to prevent this situation from arising. This prohibition is easy enough to define if it is confined to the clergyman's acceptance of a political mandate or his taking part in an election campaign. He can, however, avoid the prohibition altogether if he is given leave of absence from his official pastoral duties during his election campaign and if he ceases to practise as a parish pastor either permanently or temporarily after his election success and his appointment to a political function.

The situation becomes more problematical if he takes part in political debate or controversy that is strictly related to a theme. Is he acting politically or is he motivated by pastoral concern for the Church and his fellow-Christians when he takes an initiative as a citizen and takes part in political activity precisely as a member of the clergy? This has, after all, happened with increasing frequency in recent years in the German-speaking countries, for example, in the participation of clergy in political campaigns for more children's playgrounds and against the building of nuclear reactors and power stations, disposal points for nuclear waste and new airports. The politicians and parties attacked on such occasions and those responsible for these political decisions have often retaliated by criticising the 'political padres' for going beyond the limits of their office and neglecting their pastoral duties.

3. CHURCH DISCIPLINARY LAW AND PENALTIES IMPOSED FOR DISSENT

Special Church disciplinary courts are responsible in Germany and Austria for resolving conflicts of this kind as they arise.[4] Only a historical explanation can satisfactorily account for their existence and their detailed way of proceeding, which is strongly reminiscent of the State penal system. The influence of the particular penal jurisdiction that was considered appropriate for a State Church which was subject to the ruling prince of the German *Land* in question can still be detected. The advances made in the penal system of jurisdiction as applied to lay officials employed by the State, the most important perhaps of which is that no penalty can be imposed unless a concrete penal enactment threatening that punishment has previously been passed, have not yet been achieved in the Church's disciplinary law. The disciplinary law to which State employees are subject has at least to some extent been made more flexible and it is possible that at least a beginning has been made to refashion the Church's disciplinary jurisdiction in a theologically justifiable way.

It has to be admitted that the cases in which the disciplinary laws of the Church have been publicly applied have been more to do with imposing penalties for divorce among the clergy than with dealing with political activity. Any discussion with politically motivated members of the clergy, however, will reveal that knowledge of the existence of the Church's penal system and even the merest hint that it might possibly be applied are often sufficient to nip any desire to transgress the 'pastoral duty to remain politically discreet' in the bud.

4. REMOVAL FROM OFFICE 'IN THE INTEREST OF DUTY'— A PROBLEMATICAL WAY

A minister of the Church may often be acting overzealously and without reflection when he opens himself up to attack in respect of the choice of the weapons which he wants to use in a 'political' sermon or when he advocates certain political objectives which lie outside his normal pastoral duties. If he takes up a social or ethical position in the pulpit, this should cause scandal to no one in the congregation and if he takes part in a peaceful demonstration he should not wear his ecclesiastical robes or occupy houses or Churches. However careful he may be, however, to avoid these and other cruder forms of expression, a member of the clergy can still make himself unpopular because of his undisguised political views. Even if he commits no offence against his duties as a pastor and does not disturb the basis of trust between himself and those to whom he ministers, his dissent may still not be without professional risks in the eyes of the Church's law.

(*a*) The Concept 'In the Interest of Duty'

In the new laws in the Protestant Churches governing the duties of pastors, forms of laws based on the canon law of the Church have been included. According to these forms of law, a pastor can be removed from his office and his appointment even if he has been dutifully exercising his office and even because he has been doing so. The measures applied in such cases are said to be for 'the removal from office in the interest of duty'.[5] The essential point of this regulation is that there is no need for a member of the clergy to have committed any specifiable misdemeanour for him to be removed from his living. All that is necessary is that his 'successful activity' in his community appears to have become impossible or unlikely. The decision to remove him is usually taken by the highest Church administrative body, and the officially appointed representatives or the chairman of the Church community are often required to propose that this decision be taken or to give their consent to it. The clergyman who has been removed in this way can be transferred or elected to another parish and, if this fails or if it appears in advance to be unfeasible, he must, if necessary, either accept temporary duties or early retirement.

It cannot be denied that such measures are at least to some extent justified. It is, after all, true to say that, according to the Gospel, the pastor or minister is there for the sake of the parish community and not the community for the sake of the pastor. If there is conflict that cannot be otherwise resolved in human terms, it is better for the pastor to give way than for the community to allow itself to be pressurised by a pastor who has lost any possibility of acting effectively. A pastor who, without any fault on his part and with a clear conscience, finds himself in such a position, perhaps because of his theological or his social ethical convictions, is often reluctant to give up his living voluntarily in the community that does not want to keep him, despite the fact that he is urged to do so. He may regard it as a demand made by the Gospel and imposed on him by his ordination vow to remain in a situation of tension and to persist in his dissent. The most benign interpretation that can be placed on his reluctant transfer to another living in such circumstances is that the Church leaders want to spare him the burden of having to persist in an unpleasant situation and, to do so, take the decision on themselves to relieve him of the responsibility.

On the other hand, however, a transfer of this kind can also be a very convenient way of prematurely breaking off a debate, which may be spiritually necessary, by making use of dissent. This may result in what appears from the outside to be a truce, when in reality only a continuation of what is certainly an embarrassing controversy can hold out hope that there will eventually be mutual understanding or at least mutual toleration.

(b) The Procedure

Unfortunately, 'removals in the interest of duty' of this kind are arranged as private rather than as public procedures conducted by the Church authorities and by enactments that do not require any judicial justification. The apparent absence of any such procedure is extenuated to only a limited degree by the fact that the chairman and members of the Church or parish council must be previously given a hearing. At the same time, however, the mere fact that all these people in authority meet together in this way may point to an escalation of the conflict, which should, it needs hardly to be said, be avoided if possible.

The situation is similar with regard to the possibility that has recently been discussed in Germany, namely that the decision taken by the parish Church leaders to transfer a clergyman from one parish to another should be reviewed by the administrative court of the Church in the *Land* in question. This is, after all, because certain offences against the law of the Church can, in the case of such an appeal, even lead to the annulment of the disputed decision. The way in which the Church leaders exercise their judgment, however—and it is this that we have to consider above all here—is regularly excluded from the process of review conducted by the Church's administrative court.

The cases in which 'removals in the interest of duty' of this kind are applied are generally speaking not made public as such, nor are they usually discussed in public. It is therefore not possible for me to say here how widely this possibility is in fact exploited in order to overcome dissent within the Church. We should not, on the other hand, underestimate the effect that the existence of this measure and the fact that it is used at least from time to time can have on members of the parish clergy. They must, after all, reckon with the distinct possibility that such a procedure may be used as the result of certain modes of behaviour. In some cases, conflicts have been resolved by means of a voluntary removal that has taken place within the forms of law available. In others, members of the clergy have had to be prematurely silent and even to give way to the representatives of their parish community. Both attitudes go back to fear that they will be made the object of such a procedure for compulsory removal, without any attempt to go more deeply, even if more lengthily, into the theological questions involved in the affair.

5. THE PROCEDURES USED IN THE CHURCH IN CASES OF DEVIATION FROM THE CHURCH'S DOCTRINES

Since the turn of the century, almost all the Churches in the various German *Länder* have introduced a change in their laws which is of particular interest to us in our consideration of this question of dissent within the Church. The dissent in this instance is explicitly related to questions connected with the Church's doctrine and it is expressed particularly in cases in which ordained ministers teach doctrines and make statements about faith which differ from scriptural pronouncements. The feeling has, however, grown in recent years that one should not punish a member of the clergy for a teaching method that he uses constantly, even if what he says may be regarded as heretical or schismatical.

The Churches in each German *Land* have made use of 'laws governing objections to doctrine',[6] which partly differ from each other in characteristic details. In this way, they have devised modes of procedure to enable them to deal with cases of doctrinal dissent within the Church. All these procedures make provision for the fact that an attempt to effect a reconciliation should be made by making use of the method of individual conversations, conducted with pastoral concern, whenever a minister of the Church, while carrying out the public duties of his office in the Church, dissents from the basic principles of his Church's faith and confession of that faith. If this attempt fails, experts should then be invited by the Church to take part in a further attempt to approach the minister in question and to understand his concern and intention and, if possible, to being about a reconciliation in this way. If this also fails, a procedure which is in many ways similar to a legal procedure is then followed before a special committee responsible for passing a verdict. If this committee should decide that the clergyman in question has in fact deviated in certain important respects from the Church's teaching, that verdict will be that he must lose his living and the authority of his office in the Church. All that he will retain will be the pension that he has earned.

However many widely different theological opinions may be expressed in the German Evangelical Church today, very few occasions have arisen in the past fifty or more years when this procedure has been used. The sentences passed on these few occasions have not caused a schism in the Church, nor have they given much satisfaction to anyone. No permanent solution has been found to the doctrinal problems to which they have drawn attention. This experience, together with the costly legal proceedings involved in these procedures have also undoubtedly contributed to the fact that there has, in recent years, been very little eagerness to embark on such procedures in cases of deviation from the Church's teaching and that other methods have on the whole been preferred.

One lesson can, however, be learnt from the history of the German Evangelical Church's laws and procedures governing deviations from its teaching. It is that it has become increasingly clear that it is not possible to deal satisfactorily, in terms of the Gospel itself, in any case of dissent that has arisen in the Evangelical Church, that is, the Church of the Gospel, unless there has been a fairly long period of discussion on both sides. It is certainly to be hoped that this fundamental lesson will also be learnt in other spheres, apart from that of the procedures used in dealing with deviations from the Church's teaching. This applies in particular to the regulations governing disciplinary procedures and the removal of clergy in the Evangelical Church. These are urgently in need of reform and they are open to serious criticism in the light of the Gospel if their legal form and their practical application persist unchanged despite the advances that have been made in our knowledge both of ecclesiastical law and of theology gained in the procedure followed in cases of deviation from the Church's teaching. It is ultimately only in this way that the code of law of the Evangelical Church will serve a wider and deeper understanding of the simple fact that conflicts in the Church of the Gospel are not inevitably great misfortunes, especially if they lead to procedures in which misunderstandings are cleared up, and that a Church which contains many individual members who are critical is better off than one that is unleavened by critical thinking.[7]

Translated by David Smith

Notes

1. For this idea of the law of the German Evangelical Church, see A. Stein *Evangelisches Kirchenrecht* (Neuwied 1980) pp. 15-19.

2. For a sociological view that is very prevalent today, see Yorick Spiegel 'Pfarrer' in Gert Otto *Praktisch-theologisches Handbuch* (Hamburg ²1975) pp. 459-475.

3. For further texts and statements, see above, note 1, and Herbert Frost *Strukturprobleme evangelischer Kirchenverfassungen* (Göttingen 1972).

4. See the work cited in note 1, p. 114f. See also A. Stein 'Schuld und Vergebung im kirchlichen Amtsrecht' *Evangelische Theologie* 36 (Munich 1976) 85-94; *ibid.* 'Braucht die Kirche noch ein Disziplinarrecht?' *Amt und Gemeinde* 32 (Vienna 1981) 107-112.

5. See Hermann Weber 'Versetzungsbefugnis nach § 71 des Pfarrergesetzes der VELKD' *Zeitschrift für evangelisches Kirchenrecht* 15 (Tübingen 1970) 20-59. For a parallel in Catholic Canon Law, see Can. 2147, § 1, § 2, 2⁰-3⁰; Johannes Neumann *Grundriss des katholischen Kirchenrechtes* (Darmstadt 1981) 212f.

6. See A. Stein *Probleme evangelischer Lehrbeanstandung* (Bonn 1967); *id.* 'Evangelische Lehrordnung als Frage kirchenrechtlicher Verfahrensgestaltung' *Zeitschrift für evangelisches Kirchenrecht* 19 (Tübingen 1974) 253-275; *id.* 'Weitere Entwicklungen im Lehrrecht' *ibid.* 26 (1981) 77-79, which includes further statements.

7. Statements of this kind were made to the synods of their respective Churches in 1981 by Helmut Hild and Gerhard Brandt, who are the presidents of the assemblies of the Church in Hessen-Nassau and Rheinland respectively. Hermann Dembrowski's article, 'Plädoyer für einen guten Streit', *Evangelische Kommentare* 6 (Stuttgart 1973) 624-626, is worth reading in this context.

PART III

Dissent and Reaction in the History of the Church

Francine Cardman

Cyprian and Rome: The Controversy over Baptism

MADE BISHOP of Carthage 'while still a neophyte', Cyprian brought to that office the experience and perspective of a well-born, well-educated, and well-respected pagan.[1] Early encounters with dissent in his own see—opposition from a small but persistent group of presbyters that had objected to his election, controversy over the discipline of a group of virgins—contributed to his emerging theory of the Church and the authority of bishops. In its developed form that theory would ultimately prove inadequate to the complexities of third-century Church life, leaving Cyprian in vehement opposition to the policies and teaching of the Bishop of Rome even as he sought to remain in communion with him. During his brief episcopal career (248-258) Cyprian was several times confronted with the necessity of tempering his most deeply held convictions about the nature of the Church and the unity of its episcopacy, faith, and sacraments, with realistic appraisals of concrete situations and their limited possibilities for action. His theory of the Church required unanimity in faith and practice; his pastoral experience and ecclesiastical politics demanded diversity; and his instinctive feeling for the see of Rome caught him up in a conflict with its bishop which he was unable to resolve.

In examining the experience of Cyprian and the North African church *vis-à-vis* Rome, I begin with a brief exposition of *Cyprian's understanding of the unity of the Church*, followed by a survey of several *incidents and controversies* which shaped his thought and patterns of action. With this context established I then take up *the controversy with Stephen of Rome* over the baptism of schismatics and heretics, concluding with some final reflections on Cyprian and Rome.

1. THEORY AND PRACTICE

(a) **The Unity of the Church in theory**

The Church, for Cyprian, is one. It was founded on Peter, the source and symbol of its unity, and is constituted by its bishops, each of whom possesses the authority and the chair of Peter.[2] Though the bishops are many, the episcopal authority is one; each bishop holds his part of that authority in totality in his own see.[3] Although a bishop is finally responsible to God alone, the range of his actions is nevertheless limited by the need to preserve the unity of the Church through the communion of its bishops.[4] The one Church maintains the unity of the spirit in the bond of peace (Eph. 4:3) and is held together by charity and concord (*Ep.* 54.1).

There is, therefore, one flock and one shepherd, one spouse of Christ, one Passover and Eucharist, one seamless robe of Christ, one ark of Noah in which humankind is saved.[5] Within the one Church the see of Rome is significant as a centre and to some extent an efficacious sign of unity. For this reason the Roman Church can rightly be termed *ecclesia principalis* and, in a twofold sense, *cathedra Petri* (59.4). But, it must be noted, Cyprian in *no* way allows for a *primacy* of the Bishop of Rome in his theory of the Church. Peter's primacy was temporal, not juridical, and did not extend by succession to those who followed him in the Roman see. His importance was as the starting point, not the object, of unity.[6]

In its faith and in its sacramental life the Church depends on this fundamental unity and the power of the Holy Spirit for its holiness and for the efficacy of its sacraments. Both schism and heresy break the unity and peace of the Church, thus putting their perpetrators outside its bounds. Those who have broken with the Church, their mother, have broken also with Christ and cannot have God as their Father; neither do they possess the Holy Spirit nor the sacraments (55.24; 74.7; *Unit.* 6). That there can be *no baptism outside the Church* is clear to Cyprian even before his conflict with Rome over the validity of schismatic and heretical baptism. Just as there is one starting point of the Church, so there is but one starting point of faith.[7]

In regard to its sacramental life, its ecclesiastical structure, and its teaching, there could be for Cyprian no choice between the empirical Church and the workings of the Holy Spirit.[8] Unanimity among bishops was for him a given: 'For there could not be among us a diverse feeling in whom there was one spirit; and therefore it is manifest that he does not hold the truth of the Holy Spirit with the rest, whom we observe to think differently' (68.5).

(*b*) Diversity in Practice

Because Cyprian refused to choose between the Church and the Spirit, he worked out a pastoral and political practice which *allowed for diversity, change of mind, even dissent*, in matters of discipline and sacramental theology. *Fabian*, the Bishop of Rome (236-250), was martyred almost immediately at the beginning of the Decian persecution; Cyprian retired into hiding the better to shepherd the flock that remained behind at Carthage. In an exchange of letters with the Roman presbyters, Cyprian is at pains to justify his actions and secure their approval (7; 9; 20). Initially *opposed to the reconciliation of those who had apostasised during the persecution*, Cyprian gradually came to affirm that the lapsed not only could but should be readmitted to communion after a period of penance supervised by the bishop. In dealing with the *lapsi* Cyprian attempted to coordinate his policy with Rome's, opposing both those in Carthage who demanded immediate reconciliation (upon recommendation of a confessor) and those schismatics in Rome who followed *Novatian* in refusing readmission to the lapsed (30; 35; 36).

Novatian and his party chose schism, as did the party of Felicissimus and Fortunatus in Carthage, though for quite contrary reasons. Cyprian, for his part, chose unity. Acknowledging the precedent of certain North African bishops who had refused to allow the reconciliation of adulterers, yet had remained in communion with their co-bishops who did so (55.21), Cyprian nevertheless preferred to modify his own position—as much in accord with the opinion of Rome, one suspects, as with the constraints of compassion. He therefore reported to the Roman bishop *Cornelius*

(251-253) that he had 'submitted to the necessity of the times' (55.7). So far had his practical position gone beyond his understanding of the holiness of the Church and of those who share in its sacramental life, that he could later inform Cornelius, 'I remit everything' (59.16).

(c) The Limits of Diversity

But there were limits to diversity and limits to dissent, even for Cyprian. Schism could not be tolerated because it breaks the unity of the episcopate and the peace of the Catholic Church. Cyprian therefore excommunicated the rebellious Felicissimus and his faction in Carthage and approved Rome's refusal of recognition to the schismatics; proceeded cautiously with recognition of Cornelius as Bishop of Rome in the face of a rival claim to the episcopate by Novatian; exhorted dissident Roman confessors to return to the unity of the Church and congratulated their bishop when they had done so; and launched a full-scale campaign against the schismatic Novatian. Although—and in a sense because—Cyprian 'remits everything' to the laity, he set strict limits in regard to the clergy, particularly the bishops.

Lapsed bishops could not be readmitted to the clergy since they would contaminate the people with the 'sacrilegious sacrifices' of their 'profane altars' (68.2; 67.3, 9). So intent was Cyprian on maintaining a level of holiness in the clergy that he was willing to gainsay the decision of the Roman bishop Stephen in the case of two lapsed Spanish bishops who had sought reinstatement to their sees. The Spanish episcopacy appealed the decision to Cyprian in his role as metropolitan bishop of North Africa. Cyprian responded by instructing the clergy and people of Spain to refuse communion with the two (67).

Similarly, he felt it within his rights and responsibilities to admonish Stephen about his episcopal duties in regard to a schismatic bishop in Arles. In this case Cyprian bluntly directed Stephen to inform the bishops of Gaul and the church at Arles of the excommunication of the bishop and the consequent need to replace him (68). Taken together these incidents illustrate the limits of Cyprian's toleration for dissent, on the one hand, and the latitude of his dealings with the Bishop of Rome on the other.

2. THE BAPTISMAL CONTROVERSY

As Bishop of Carthage it was natural for Cyprian to be responsive to the opinion and approval of Rome. What was probably unclear even to himself, however, was the extent to which he also felt *responsible to Rome*.[9] His inchoate sense of responsibility to Rome did not, in any case, prevent him from coaxing, contradicting, or even castigating its bishop as the occasion required. When the question arose in 255 of how to treat those followers of Novatian who wished to enter or return to the Catholic Church, Cyprian found himself caught in the middle of the unresolved ambiguities of his own theory and practice. His subsequent actions appear paradoxical, at best.

Because he considered agreement on matters of faith to be crucially important for the Church, when it came to a question about baptism, the very beginning of the faith, he disagreed in the strongest terms with Stephen of Rome and rejected his 'error' on this matter (74.1). Because the unity and integrity of the Church were likewise critical, Cyprian sacrificed the consistency of his own understanding of the Holy Spirit's role in the Church and sacraments for the sake of the unity of the episcopate.[10] And because apostolic tradition, custom, and 'ancient usage' (45.3) were of value to him, he opposed truth and reason to custom and error in defence of the Gospel (71.3; 73.13; 74.9). What brought him to this pass and what were the consequences of his conflict with Stephen?

In surveying the baptismal controversy, *three parties and points of view* need to be taken into account: *Stephen*, Bishop of Rome from 254 to 257; *Firmilian*, Bishop of Caesarea in Cappadocia; and *Cyprian*. After analysing their positions on schismatic or heretical baptism and the authority to which they appealed, I will explore some of the consequences of the controversy.

(a) The Question and the Points of View

The question of how to deal with schismatics or heretics who wished to enter or reenter the Church was essentially a question of the *validity of baptism outside the Church*. All three parties to the dispute agreed that those who had already been baptised in the Catholic Church and then abandoned it for heresy or schism could be received back into communion by the laying on of hands, as in the case of penitents. What was in dispute was whether those who had been baptised in heresy or schism were to be received in the same manner or whether they had first to be baptised in the Church.[11]

Stephen held that baptism in the name of Jesus Christ was valid baptism, whether performed inside or outside the Church (73.16; 74.5; 75.7, 9, 11). 'The name of Christ,' he is quoted as arguing, 'is of great advantage to faith and the sanctification of baptism; so that whoever anywhere is baptised in the name of Christ, immediately obtains the grace of Christ' (75.18). Stephen claimed for his position the authority of apostolic tradition and custom, rejecting the decisions of the Synod of Carthage in 255 with the remark that 'nothing [should be] innovated which has not been handed down' (74.1). He apparently also appealed to a specifically Roman tradition (75.5, 6, 19) and seems to have claimed the authority of Peter and Paul (71.3; 75.6) as well as a special authority for his episcopal see as the successor of Peter (75.17).[12]

Both Firmilian and Cyprian opposed Stephen's view and rejected his Petrine pretensions. They held that baptism *outside the Church* was *no baptism* at all, so that schismatics and heretics wanting to enter the Church had first to be baptised. Lacking the unity of the Church and, therefore, the power of the Holy Spirit, schismatics and heretics could only work futility and falsehood; nothing done by them could be approved by the Church (70.3).

Firmilian claimed for his church and those of Cappadocia, Cilicia, Galatia and neighbouring provinces the authority of unbroken observance of a tradition handed down from Christ and the apostles, that there was 'one church of God and one holy baptism' (75.19). He cites the synod of Iconium (*c.* 230), which had rejected all baptism outside the Church as further evidence of this tradition. He is aware, too, that the North Africans had not always held their present opinion, but had forsaken custom after learning the truth (75.19).

Cyprian acknowledged that he could not call on a long tradition of practice, since North Africa had only broken with the Roman custom a generation or so earlier ('long since', he says).[13] Instead he had to appeal to the claims of reason and the basic sense of the Gospel in order to argue that, 'It has been delivered to us that there is one God, one Christ, one hope, one faith, one Church, and one baptism ordained only in the one Church . . .' (74.11). It is instructive here to observe Cyprian's rejection of custom in favour of reason (71.3) and the truth of revelation (73.13; 74.9). His attack on Stephen's opinion as merely a 'human tradition' (74.3) led him to the conclusion that 'custom without truth is the antiquity of error' (74.9).

(b) The Ending of the Conflict

How did the parties to this confrontation react and what was its eventual outcome?

Stephen was indignant and insistent. According to Firmilian he had broken peace with the eastern churches and had refused to receive bishops whom Cyprian had sent to him as messengers, denying them the hospitality of the Roman Church as well (75.6, 25). Firmilian angrily labels him 'an apostate from the communion of ecclesiastical unity' (75.24). Cyprian inquires sarcastically whether Stephen could be said to glorify God, since he, 'a friend of heretics and an enemy to Christians, thinks that the priests of God, who support the truth of Christ and the unity of the Church, are to be excommunicated (*abstinendos*)' (74.8).

On the basis of these assertions it seems likely that Stephen had at least temporarily broken communion with Cyprian and the church of Carthage, as well as with the churches of Asia Minor.[14] Firmilian, for his part, was outraged, declaring that Stephen had cut himself off from a great many churches by his actions: 'For while you think that all may be excommunicated by you, you have excommunicated yourself alone' (75.24). Cyprian, on the other hand, was both cautious and conflicted. He was convinced that Stephen was in error and held an 'evil and false position' (74.1, 10), but thought that he could be persuaded by reason to change his mind ('a bishop should learn as well as teach'). He regretted and rebuked Stephen's obstinacy and presumption' (74.3, 7, 10). He unhesitatingly reported to Stephen the decisions of Carthaginian Synods that flatly contradicted his position (e.g., 72).[15] He accused Stephen of supporting heretics against the Church (69.10; 73.10, 26; 74.1). But coercion was distasteful to him and he refused to compel agreement with his views, whether from Stephen or the North African bishops.[16] Whatever Stephen's actions in regard to excommunication, Cyprian seems not to have broken the peace of communion from his side.

After the council at Carthage in September, 256, there is no further mention of the baptismal controversy in Cyprian's correspondence.

The conflict simply ends without any real resolution. Stephen died a martyr in August, 257, at the start of Valerian's renewal of persecution, Cyprian in September, 258, after a period of self-imposed exile. Robert Evans' observation on the situation is apt: 'the crisis seems carefully to have been ignored but not forgotten, the Africans continuing into the fourth century their practice of baptising schismatics.'[17] Only then, in exchange for Roman support against a schismatic rival, would the current Bishop of Carthage embrace Rome's sacramental theology; and only during the episcopate of Augustine (396-430) would that fourth century schism of the Donatists, who looked to Cyprian for the legitimacy of their theology, be dealt a decisive blow.

Why did Cyprian not break with Stephen, drawing the *logical conclusion* from his opposition to Stephen's sacramental theology and its implications for ecclesiology? H. von Campenhausen attributes it to Cyprian's 'naive ecclesiasticising of Christian life'.[18] G. S. M. Walker cites Cyprian's need for communion with Rome, despite his willingness to disagree with its bishop.[19] M. Sage credits his recognition of the hopelessness of changing Stephen's mind.[20] And M. Bevenot perhaps comes the closest to the truth when he points to the 'blind spot' Cyprian had in regard to Rome and his inability to comprehend that his practice had outrun his theory.[21]

To Bevenot's perceptive remarks I want only to add a few suggestions about how that blind spot functioned in the baptismal controversy. Along with his instinctive sense of the real as well as the symbolic importance of Rome, Cyprian had to reckon with his own intense dislike of schism. His experience with the *lapsi* had led him to a view of the Church as a mixed body, composed of wheat and tares, in which it was difficult if not impossible to distinguish the two on the basis of human judgment (54.3; 55.25, 27). Perhaps he had also learned a certain *tolerance for the ambiguity and complexity of human and ecclesial existence*. It is also quite likely that Cyprian had to face the political realities of the situation and avoid isolating himself to such an extent that he would cut himself off from the rest of the Church, thereby falling into the kind of *de facto* excommunication with which Firmilian had charged Stephen. And, finally, Cyprian may well have had in mind his own responsibility before God, to whom one day he, like every bishop, would have to render an account.

Notes

1. The phrase is his biographer's: Pontius, *Vita*, 5. Both M. Sage, *Cyprian*, Patristic Monograph Series, no. 1 (Cambridge, Ma.: The Philadelphia Patristics Foundation, Ltd., 1975) 330, and R. Evans *One and Holy: The Church in Latin Patristic Thought* (London 1972) 47-49, comment on the influence of the models and style of Roman administration on the Christian episcopacy as more members of the upper classes became bishops.

2. Ep. 3.3; 59.14; 70.3; 73.11; *De unitate*, 4-5. Cyprian's works are edited by W. Hartel in CSEL III, i-iii, English translation in The Ante-Nicene Fathers, vol. 5, A. Roberts and J. Donaldson, eds., 1886. Hereafter letters will be cited according to Hartel's numbering, by number and section in parentheses in the text. For scholarly disputes on *De unitate*, 4 (the so-called 'primacy' text), as well as for the generally accepted interpretation, see M. Bevenot, '*Primatus Petro Datur*: St Cyprian on the Papacy' *J. Th. St.*, n.s. 5 (1954) 19-35.

3. *De unitate*, 5-6; M. Bevenot '*In Solidum* and St Cyprian: A Correction' *J. Th. St.*, n.s. 6 (1955) 244-248.

4. M. Bevenot 'A Bishop is Responsible to God Alone (St Cyprian)' *Rech. Sci. Rel.* 39/40 (1951/52) *Mélanges Jules Lebreton* I, 397-415.

5. For these images of the Church's unity, see *De unitate*, 6-8; Ep. 69.4-6; 74.11; and Firmilian's use of them in 75.14-15.

6. Considerable controversy has centred on the question of the Roman primacy in Cyprian. See Bevenot 'Primatus'; Evans 'One and Holy', cited in note 1, 48-55; A. Demoustier 'Épiscopat et union a Rome selon Saint Cyprien' *Rech. Sci. Rel.* 52 (1964) 337-369; J. Quasten *Patrology* (Westminster, Md. 1953) 375-378; H. Koch *Cyprian und der römische Primat*, *T.U.* 35, hft. 1 (Leipzig 1910).

7. For Cyprian's use of trinitarian similes (learned from Tertullian) to explain unity and multiplicity, see Evans, in the work cited in note 1, 52-55.

8. *Ibid.* 61.

9. Irenaeus *Adv. Haer.*, III. 3.1-2 and Tertullian *De praescriptione* 36, for the relationship of Carthage to Rome and other cities to nearby major episcopal sees. Bevenot 'Primatus' 35, and 'Bishop' 415, remarks on Cyprian's inability to explain the particular hold that Rome had on him in practice.

10. Evans, in the work cited in note 1, 61-64; G. S. M. Walker *The Churchmanship of St Cyprian*, Ecumenical Studies in History, no. 9 (Richmond, Va. 1969) 18.

11. Cyprian acknowledges the practice of receiving as penitents those who had gone over to schism or heresy and then returned to the Church, but he chides Stephen for confusing that situation with the case of those baptised *outside* the Church: 71.2. Throughout the controversy there seems to have been some confusion as to whether the imposition of hands is for the sake of penitence or for the completion of baptism by the confirmation or bestowal of the Holy Spirit. See, e.g., 69.10; 74.5.

12. Firmilian cites Stephen as contending that 'he holds by succession the throne of Peter' (75.17). This text is the earliest notice of a bishop of Rome appealing explicitly to Petrine succession for his authority. See Sage, the work cited in note 1, 314.

13. 70.1, referring to decisions reached by a council under Agrippinus of Carthage, c. 218-222. See C. J. Hefele *A History of Christian Councils to A.D. 325*, 2nd ed., rev., transl. W. Clark (Edinburgh 1883) pp. 86-87.

14. Evans, the work cited in note 1, p. 61; Sage, the work cited in note 1, pp. 314, 326.

15. Three Carthaginian Councils were held on the question of baptism: Spring 255, Spring 256, and September, 256.

16. See 69.17; 73.26; and Cyprian's comments at the opening of the September, 256, council: 'each of us should bring forward what we think, judging no one, nor rejecting anyone from the right of communion, if he should think differently from us' (*Sententiae Episcoporum*).

17. The work cited in note 1, p. 61.

18. *Ecclesiastical Authority and Spiritual Power* (Stanford, Ca.: 1969; *Kirchliches Amt und geistliche Vollmacht* [Tübingen 1953]) p. 292.

19. The work cited in note 9, p. 32.

20. The work cited in note 1, pp. 312, 334.

21. 'Bishop', cited in note 4, 415.

Paolo Ricca

Sect or Order?
(Waldensians—Franciscans)

1. COMMON ORIGINS, COMMON AIMS

SECT OR ORDER? According to the judgment of the 'great' medieval Church, the Waldensians became a sect and the Franciscans an order. However, in their original inspiration and first stage of development the Waldensian *societas* and the Franciscan *fraternitas* each constituted neither a sect nor an order. They were very quickly misunderstood in this way. In 1226 the *Ursperg Chronicle* already makes a polemical distinction between the Franciscans and the Dominicans on the one hand and the Waldensians and 'Umiliati' on the other, qualifying the former as 'religious orders' and disqualifying the latter as 'sects'. It is worth quoting statements from the *Chronicle* in spite of the inaccuracies they contain.

'Towards 1212 when the world was moving towards sunset, two religious orders (two *religiones*) arose in the bosom of the Church, whose youth renews itself like the eagle's, and were confirmed by the Holy See, viz., the Friars Minor and the Preachers. No doubt these were approved at that time because two sects (two *secte*), which previously arose in Italy still exist today: they are called respectively the Umiliati and the Poor of Lyons.[1]

Immediately afterwards the Chronicler sees the Franciscans and the Waldensians as true alternatives: the pope approved the former, not independently of the latter but in their place. It is clear that the Chronicle projects onto the origins of the two movements the situation which had arisen in the second and third decades of the thirteenth century, when their relations with Rome had already crystallised: the Franciscans had been integrated into the Church as a monastic order and the Waldensians had been condemned with a 'perpetual anathema' as an heretical sect.

In reality, the better we come to know the circumstances and characters belonging to the early days of Waldensianism and Franciscanism, the more we are forced to recognise their substantial affinity.

This is true both because *Peter Waldo* and *Francis* came from the same social class, responded in a very similar way to the same vocation and adopted the same plan of

Christian life and because they both, with their followers, created a form of 'resistance' in the Church which took the form not of claiming a right but of expressing a higher form of obedience.

Resistance and surrender for Francis? Resistance with no surrender for Waldo? Possibly. But what is more important to note is that the behaviour of the first Waldensians and the first Franciscans was beyond the alternative of 'sect or order'. In their initial stage, both movements practised a fairly similar programme of *apostolic life* which, while remaining perfectly orthodox (this was true at the beginning for the Waldensians too) constituted *in fact* in the Christianity of the time a Christian *rallying point* which was not the official Church. If we do not want to call it an alternative, we may describe it as constructive opposition.

Certainly, especially with Pope *Innocent III* the situation changed radically. This may have been caused by the internal development of Waldensianism or by the fact that the pope may have grasped that a Franciscan 'order' well integrated into the Church, could be a providential antidote to the Waldensian 'sect' (and to many others) and become the ideal instrument for a new kind of fight against heresy. Side by side with pure and simple repression of heretics, they could now be combated on their own territory by imitating the positive contents of their proposals and at the same time attacking their criticisms. This new method of attack imitated the heretics in apostolic life and at the same time reproved them for failure in obedience to the hierarchy, towards which the new 'order' adopted an attitude of absolute loyalty and docility.

But at the beginning Waldensians and Franciscans fought for the same cause with the same weapons. In spite of their all too evident limitations, we may still recall today the view of the modernist historian Ernesto Buonaiuti who saw *Waldo of Lyons*, *Francis of Assisi* and *Gioacchino da Fiore* as 'a triad of great evangelical reformers', creators of what he is not afraid to call 'the first Reformation' (as distinct from the second brought about by Luther, Zwingli and Calvin in the sixteenth century).

According to Buonaiuti, Waldo, Francis and Gioacchino are figures whom 'it is impossible to separate' because together they represent 'the first yearning of the reawakened Christian conscience in the middle ages for a direct and immediate restoration of Gospel values and Christ's message'.[2] With different emphases and also different results, Waldo, Francis and Gioacchino tried to reawaken the Church through the *Gospel and the Spirit*. They did not seek partial modifications, sectarian reforms, they did not claim special rights, they merely wanted to follow the Gospel. They worked for a Christian rebirth through the Word and the Spirit. They did *not* try to create *a new monastic order, or a Church within the Church or an alternative Church*. Their chief concern was not the Church but the *Gospel within the Church*.

2. NUDI NUDUM CHRISTUM SEQUENTES: THE WALDENSIAN AIM

Today it is still not certain whether the Waldensians (who began their activity between 1173 and 1175) were anathematised at the Council of Verona in 1184 or whether this only happened later: viz., they were condemned fairly early but not immediately—which confirms the substantially orthodox nature of the first Waldensian movement.

Neither are the *reasons for their excommunication* at all clear: however, it seems certain that a fundamental reason was the Waldensian practice of preaching freely (*libere predicare*), even though they were simple lay people. The first Waldensian *societas* was a community of lay preachers. There is a famous description of the first

Waldensians made by Walter Map, a Canon of the Curia, who met some of them in Rome on the occasion of the Third Lateran Council:

> 'These people never have a fixed abode. They go about in pairs, barefoot, dressed in wool, they possess nothing, having everything in common among themselves like the apostles. Naked they follow a naked Christ. Now they begin in a very humble fashion because they cannot gain a foothold, but if we admit them, we will be driven out ourselves.'[3]

This is a description of a group of itinerant preachers who are trying to reproduce the style and content of the early Christian apostles.

We may therefore define the type of opposition offered to the Church by the early Waldensians as an opposition of laity who intentionally remained laity and whose objective was freedom to preach. The phenomenon is not an isolated one but this does not make it less significant: the Waldensians felt called by God himself to exercise a fundamental Christian function—preaching—without becoming incorporated in the Church's clerical and monastic structure. They were ministers without being either clergy or monks.

This is why Waldo himself seems to have *extended the faculty of preaching to women*. Only in a system where the clergy have a monopoly of preaching could women be excluded. When the laity become active and not just the passive recipients of preaching, its feminine component must also take part. If the laity has the right to preach, so *eo ipso* do women. It is therefore not surprising that preaching by women among the Waldensians at the end of the thirteenth century was 'a mass manifestation, the rule rather than the exception'.[4] And according to some evidence, in certain sectors of Waldensianism in the thirteenth century, women were also recognised as having the right to *preside over the celebration of the eucharist*.

The Waldensians wanted to preach without abandoning their lay status. Among them, *the laity* became the missionaries, they emerged from their subordinate condition of 'learning Church' and themselves unexpectedly *became* the teaching Church. And this was probably what caused the break with the ecclesiastical authority. At its origins Waldensianism was perfectly orthodox on the level of doctrine, but less so on the level of individuation of ecclesial subjects, as we would call them today.

The first Waldensian community was a Christocratic lay brotherhood (with no *prepositus*, in accordance with the wishes of Waldo himself, which were in fact ignored by the Lombardy Waldensians). They were a new ecclesial subject of the stage of the Christian history of the West: an interdependent laity, not led by persons belonging to the then dominant social class, the merchant bourgeoisie. The Waldensians shared with the bourgeoisie a spirit of initiative and the willingness to create new things, but—at their conversion—they renounced the capitalistic spirit through a radical choice of evangelical poverty. They were a laity with a strong sense of vocation and missionary spirit, they were prepared to sacrifice everything in order really to *follow Christ* in the literal sense. This was the precondition for their fundamental work of preaching the Gospel in the vernacular (in practice this was a biblical literacy campaign), with particular stress on the works that Jesus recommended his disciples to do in the Sermon on the Mount, because these alone validate the Christian community as a community whose 'righteousness' exceeds that of the scribes and pharisees (see Matt. 5:20).

Obviously the ecclesiastical authorities were frightened by this Waldensian initiative—in spite of their proven initial doctrinal orthodoxy—and they were quickly excluded from the communion of the 'great Church'. What were the authorities afraid of? The seizing of authority away from the clergy, the monastic life and the hierarchy? However, it does not look as if the early Waldensians had aims of this sort. Their initiative did not take away authority from the clergy but it was a *reassessment of the clergy* (accentuated by the Donatist conception of the ministry held by the Lombardy Waldensians and later by the whole movement). It is a fact that Waldo and his followers maintained in relation to ecclesiastical authority 'oportet Deo obedire magis quam hominibus', which demonstrated that they possessed, as laity, a very high sense of vocation.

Although the early behaviour of the Waldensians was neither polemical nor anti-institutional, the hierarchy must have sensed *danger* in their *societas*. Perhaps the Waldensians did not even expressly intend to do so, but they changed the traditional face of the Church which was entirely, or almost entirely, in the hands of the clergy. They gained for the 'simple laity' new and broader room for manoeuvre in the field of the prophetic ministry of the Church. They recognised ecclesiastical authority but it was no longer the last resort: *obedience to God did not necessarily coincide with obedience to the hierarchy*. In the Waldensian conscience the requirement to preach is stronger than fear of disciplinary sanctions. Beyond their subjective will, Waldensianism contained 'an objectively subversive demand'.[5] The Church of the time preferred to expel them from the area of orthodoxy, perhaps especially because this lay brotherhood of itinerant preachers with the Bible in their hands claimed a certain autonomy of vocation in relation to the hierarchy, which forced them to modify their own view of themselves and of their role in the Church.

It would have been difficult for *societas* of Waldensians, with their emphasis on the *centrality of the Bible* in missionary work, to be integrated into the medieval Church, without changing their original nature. Or if they had been, the consequences for the medieval Church would have been very great indeed. In fact the Waldensian right of opposition came up against the even stronger right of excommunication, on which the hierarchy held a monopoly.

The dialogue between Waldensianism and the 'great Church' did not last long and after the break the division became wider and wider, until they were poles apart. However, even in the mid-fifteenth century the Waldensian bishop and martyr Frederick Reiser, expressed himself thus before the tribunal of the opposition: 'Frederick, by the grace of God, bishop of the believers in the Roman Church who disdain the donation of Constantine.'[6] Here Waldensianism is still seen as a movement within the Church. But the Church had not seen it that way for a long time. In the case of the Waldensians, there had proved to be too little room within the Church for the exercise of a real right of opposition.

3. LIVING SECUNDUM FORMAM SANCTI EVANGELII: FRANCIS'S AIM

Francis also belonged to the world of the *nudi nudum Christum sequentes*. This was shown in an emblematic manner in the famous dramatic scene in which he stripped naked in front of the bishop, his family and a large crowd and returned his clothes and money to his father. It was the decisive break with his world and his past—a kind of figurative stripping off of the old man (see Col. 3:10) and the decisive step towards a new *forma vitae* which would positively express his conversion. As we read in the *Testament* of 1226, 'After the Lord gave me brothers, no one showed me what I ought to do, but the Most High himself revealed to me that I should *live in accordance with the form of the holy Gospel*'. This information is important for various reasons.

Firstly, it was only after Francis had collected the first group of 'brothers' around himself that he faced the problem of a 'form of life': *it was a community rather than a personal need*. The community preceded the rule and not vice versa. In fact Francis was seeking for more than a rule, he was seeking a 'form of life', a way of being: what form and hence what content could or should a Christian community have? The answer came from above. It is very significant that at the end of his life Francis ascribes his initiative directly and solely to divine inspiration, without any ecclesiastical mediation.

Francis, then, realised that he was starting something new, both with respect to the great Christian tradition and with respect to the various ecclesial forms of association in his time. A new community was born which was neither clerical nor monastic, nor purely a lay community. Francis welcomed both laymen, like himself and clergy, *uniting all together in the single fundamental bond of brotherhood*. The community's programme was 'to live in accordance with the form of the Gospel'. In the words of the Unratified Rule (1221): 'This is the life of the Gospel of Jesus Christ which Brother Francis asked the Lord Pope Innocent to allow and confirm.' The Franciscan community thus made the Gospel their rule of life.

This choice, both elementary and radical, absolutely orthodox and secretly revolutionary, was not in any polemical relation to the other *forma vitae* mentioned in the *Testament*: that of the bishops who 'live in accordance with the form of the holy Roman Church'. Francis repeatedly, almost obstinately, confessed his unshakeable 'faith' in them, 'because of their ordination' (thus setting himself against the Donatist tendencies or positions present in the heterodox movements of his time and perhaps also in a certain popular base). The Franciscan choice was therefore entirely and purposely confined within the boundaries of the Church of Rome, towards whom (and towards whose ministers, from the pope to the lowest priest), Francis adopted an attitude of unconditional loyalty.

However, *within* the Roman Church which had its own form of life, Francis chose a different form of life: to live the Gospel, that is, to live the life of Christ. It is obvious that the two forms of life do not coincide: if they did, Francis would not have needed a divine revelation in order to adopt his way; he would have found it in the Church. On the other hand, it is also obvious that Francis does not set one against the other. He insists with equal vigour on the need to 'live and speak in a Catholic way' (Unratified Rule 19) and on the need to keep the *Rule* (*Testament*), *that is the Gospel*, 'simply and without comment'.

We could describe Francis's *programme* as *Catholic-evangelical*. He tried to be fully Catholic on the level of faithfulness to the Church and fully evangelical on the level of faithfulness to the 'life of the Gospel of Jesus Christ'.[7] Therefore it is, to put it mildly, unilateral and ultimately misleading to present Francis as 'ecclesiality personified' ('personifizierte Kirchlichkeit').[8] It would be closer to the reality to describe him as '*evangelicity personified*'.

Precisely because of this 'personified evangelicity' Francis and his community offered a *model of Christian authenticity and thus a living challenge to the Church and especially its leadership*. It is therefore not surprising that the *Leggenda perugina* attributes this remark to Francis: '. . . I intend above all to convert the prelates with humility and respect'.[9] It was thus inevitable that Francis' double loyalty—to the Church and to the Gospel—should create strong tensions in the Order and in the Church and objective contradictions, even beyond the subjective will of the protagonists.

Thus, for example, the radical choice of poverty and begging (although the latter was practised in the case of necessity) was a kind of 'mystical strike' (Bonaiuti) not only against the feudal regime of the Church and, more generally, the economic forms in operation at the time, but also against the accumulation of capital by the free monastic co-operatives after the Cistercian reform. Analogously, Chapter 16 of the *Unratified Rule* on the brothers who 'go among the Saracens and other heathens', both confirms the fundamental missionary and evangelising vocation of the first Franciscan community and objectively constitutes an antithesis to the Crusade which, as is well known, was the central nucleus of papal politics at the time. It is not accidental that in the *Ratified Rule* of 1223 this chapter is somewhat mutilated and shorn of those parts that made it an alternative to the politics of the Crusades.

Furthermore, the original Franciscan community was a *fraternitas sui generis*,[10] *alien to the clerical models and juridical spirit, wholly concerned with the following of the 'lowly' ('minor') Christ*, the servant. It was governed by the great evangelical principle of the turning upside down of hierarchies as in Matt. 20:20-27 (see chaps. 4, 5 and 6 of the *Unratified Rule*). Slowly but inexorably, this community which was anomalous in the religious scene of its time, was regimented into the conventual and clerical tradition and made uniform. The primitive *forma evangelii* became the *forma ecclesiae*.

What can we say? An anonymous biographer of Gregory IX wrote in about 1240 that Gregory—when he was still Cardinal Ugolino, 'protector' of the order—'gave form to that movement which was still formless'.[11] In fact the movement was not formless; it had the *forma sacti evangelii*. *The Church integrated the movement into itself without integrating itself into the movement*. On several critical issues the Church remodelled the primitive *forma vitae* of the Franciscans in its image and likeness rather than remodelling itself in the image and likeness of the Franciscan *forma vitae*. By transforming the movement into an Order, the Church adopted it, but also—to an extent difficult to indicate precisely—*neutralised* it. The Church guaranteed the movement ecclesial sanction and institutional continuity but at the same time insured itself and its own continuity.

In conclusion, in the light of what happened to the Waldensian and Franciscan movements, the question: sect or order? becomes transposed into another question: how far is the Church a space in which the Gospel understood as 'life of Jesus in community form'[12] can be fully and freely lived?

Notes

1. Text in Giovanni Gonnet, 'Le Cheminement des vaudois vers le schisme et l'heresie (1174-1218)' in *Cahiers de civilisation mediévale* (University of Poitiers) (October-December 1976) p. 315ff.

2. Ernesto Buonaiuti *Pietre miliari nella storia del cristianesimo* (Modena ²1935) pp. 176 and 177.

3. *Enchiridion Fontium Valdensium* ed. Giovanni Gonnet (Torre Pellice 1958) p. 123.

4. Gottfried Koch 'La donna nel Catarismo e nel Valdismo medievale' *Medioevo ereticale* ed. Ovidio Capitani (Bologna 1977) p. 274.

5. Giovanni Miccoli *Storia d'Italia* II/I (Turin 1974) p. 653.

6. Amedeo Molnar *Storia dei Valdesi* I (Turin 1974) p. 306 note 10.

7. See Kurt-Victor Selge 'Rechtsgestalt und Idee der frühen Gemeinschaft des Franz von Assisi: Erneuerung der einen Kirche' in *Festschrift für H. Bornkamm* (Göttingen 1966) p. 28f. On the problem of Franciscan origins, see the fine volume of Stanislao da Campagnola *Le origini francescane come problema storiografico* (Perugia ²1979).

8. The expression, coined by the Cappucin H. Felder, was adopted by Kajetan Esser OFM *Die religiöse Bewegungen des Hochmittelalters und Franziskus von Assisi: Festgabe Joseph Lortz* II (Baden-Baden 1958) p. 311.

9. *Leggenda perugina* n. 115: *Fonti Francescane* (Assisi 1978) p. 1283.

10. Jacques le Goff 'Le Vocabulaire des catégories sociales chez saint Francois d'Assise et ses biographes du XIIIe siècle' in *Ordres et classes* (Paris 1973) esp. pp. 101-107.

11. Quoted by Giovanni Miccoli, in the work cited in note 5, p. 741. On Francis and Ugolino as personfications of 'two different worlds', two different 'visions' and on the result of their meeting, see the excellent essay by Kurt-Victor Selge 'Franz von Assisi und Hugolino von Ostia' in *San Francesco nella ricerca storica degli ultimi ottanta anni* (Todi 1971) pp. 159-222.

12. This is the way Ubertino da Casale defines Franciscanism in 1305: *Fonti Francescane* (note 9), p. 1689.

Martin Brecht

A Revolt of the Church against the Church? (Luther)[1]

AS A Church historian, I think that the best way of dealing with this subject is not to write an abstract or very systematic article, but to let Martin Luther speak as far as possible for himself. He was not born a rebel. It is true that he entered a monastery against his father's will, but this was a step that he took as the result of a higher necessity. As a young professor, he was moved by genuine concern to criticise quite openly the obvious abuses in the Church of the time and he did so before the conflict was engaged, but he never wanted to be a 'Bohemian' and separate himself from that Church. He had a position of leadership in his monastic order himself and demanded a great deal of superiors and prelates. At the same time, however, he also insisted that superiors had to be obeyed by their subjects, even if they were themselves not good men and their commandments were not reasonable. In any conflict between the followers of a stricter observance and his own Order, he was firmly on the side of his superiors and urged obedience to them. He always aimed to be an obedient son of the Church.

1. THE CONTROVERSY OVER INDULGENCES

Even the great controversy did not begin as a revolt, but with a loyal letter dated 31 October 1517 and addressed to Archbishop Albrecht of Mainz, who was responsible for the distribution of the jubilee indulgence. This letter had been written on account of the misunderstandings caused among the people by those who had been preaching about the indulgence. Luther claimed that these sermons gave rise to a false sense of security with regard to salvation and forgiveness and this constituted, in his opinion, a danger to men's souls. He also insisted that the indulgence was in competition with the activity of Christian love. The instruction for the commissaries of the indulgence contained statements that were pastorally and theologically quite risky and were therefore bound to result in dissent. Luther had written this letter as a responsible member of the Church who was very conscious of his Christian duty. He deliberately signed it as a 'doctor of theology'. Included with the letter were his *Ninety-five Theses on the Power of Indulgences*.

Luther who, as a professor, was fully justified in doing so, dealt here with a second measure against the practice of indulgences in initiating a theological debate on the doctrine of indulgences, which at that time had not yet been finally defined. He believed, on the basis of the New Testament teaching, that penance was an attitude that should continue throughout the whole of the Christian's life. It was not, in his opinion, something that could be exclusively restricted to sacramental confession and satisfaction. Many questions concerning the Church's practice of sacramental confession, many of them to do with the pope's power to punish sinners, and the Church's legal power over the dead, arose as a result of this and they infringed on the papal power to grant indulgences. The only precondition for forgiveness was, Luther argued, contrition and the morality of penance was destroyed by the doctrine of indulgences.

Naturally enough, Luther took as his point of departure the fact that derogation from the activity of Christian love by the practice of indulgences was also rejected by the pope himself. The important theology of the treasure of the Church, which was closely related to the doctrine of indulgences, was also thrown into doubt. Luther was of the opinion that the only treasure that the Church had was the Gospel of the grace of God. Luther drew attention in turn to the awkward questions that the people were asking, one of them being, for example, why the pope did not stand up for the souls in purgatory simply out of love and not only on the basis of money. In their radical exposure of the pastoral and theological weaknesses and even errors contained in the doctrine of indulgences, Luther's *Ninety-five Theses* constituted a very sensitive criticism of a practice that was not entirely undisputed by the Church's leaders, but was on the whole approved by them.

2. THE CONTROVERSY OVER JUSTIFICATION

It is quite legitimate to ask whether criticism of this kind was acceptable to the Church or whether it did not have to be rejected in advance. What is in either case certain is that the questions that Luther asked were so serious and so important that they had to be considered. Luther was not in revolt against the Church. His aim was to renew the Church, but those who opposed him saw it very differently. His bishop assumed that he was attacking the power of the Church. The archbishop informed the pope. The leading commissary of the indulgence, Johann Tetzel, called him a heretic who should be burnt at the stake.

It is tragic that the central question of penance at once became the core of a fundamental conflict over authority. Whereas Luther's opponents criticised him on the basis of the conventional teaching about penance, it was the doctrine of justification that he himself developed in the course of the debate. At the centre of this doctrine was acknowledgment of *faith* in the words of forgiveness mediated by the priest as the servant of Christ. A number of far-reaching consequences resulted from this. The real strength of Luther's dissent was to be found not so much in his eloquence, cunning or intelligent argumentation, as in the insights to which his faith had access and his faith itself, without which he would hardly have been able to continue. It seems likely that the quality of dissent in the Church is ultimately to be distinguished by its inner strength rather than by its outward activities and consequences.

The conflict developed remarkably in the course of very few months. In his *Resolutions on the Theses*, which Luther wrote in the spring of 1518, but which his bishop at first asked him not to publish, he went further than his original position. He still regarded indulgences in this treatise as an evil that had to be tolerated and believed that it was possible for the pope to err. Luther knew that he had been denounced in Rome, but he still dedicated his 'Resolutions' to the pope and set out his case in this context. He made it quite clear that he did not intend to revoke what he had said, but despite this he entrusted the final decision to the pope and he declared that he would accept the pope's pronouncement as the voice of Christ and that he would die if he deserved to die. In his subsequent 'Protestation', he at once made it known that he would not accept the opinions of the canon lawyers and the scholastic theologians, including those of Thomas Aquinas especially, without putting them to the test. For a very long time, his attitude was characterised by this mixture of self-confidence and a very moving trust in the Church leaders.

3. THE TRIAL

(a) The Opening of the Trial

Luther's trial nonetheless opened in the summer of 1518 in Rome. The charge against him was suspicion of heresy and this was a little later changed to an accusation of notorious heresy. This charge was based on the opinion of Magister Sacri Palatii Sylvester Prierias, who at once asserted the following principles: the head and centre of the Church was the pope, who was infallible in his statements about faith and morals, and whoever did not adhere to the doctrines of the Roman Church and the pope as the infallible rule of faith, by which even Scripture was authorised, was a heretic.

In the concrete, this meant that any dissent with the Church's practice of indulgences was heresy. The Church could not be expected to consent to any objections, even if they were made by lay people, and Prierias devoted very little attention to these. Any further discussion of the matter seemed to have been ended by the heavy hand of authority.

The Thomist Prierias was a very partisan judge as far as Luther was concerned. The latter made a distinction from this time onwards between the apparatus of the Curia and the pope himself. He by-passed the problem of authority by contrasting his own principles and those of Prierias without making any comment. In the case of Saint Paul, Luther insisted, everything was tested against the norm of Scripture and what was good was retained. According to Augustine, he continued, only the Bible had infallible authority. The Law of the Church also made it clear that nothing could be alleged unless it was contained in Scripture. In basing himself firmly on the authority of the Bible, Luther focused attention on the conflict of norms in the Church and at the same time took it to a much deeper level.

(b) The Hearing

Because of political links with Frederick, the Elector of Saxony, Luther's case was heard by Cajetan, the papal legate, in Augsburg and not in Rome. Cajetan's task was not to engage in disputation with Luther, but rather simply to accept his recantation. What was required of the latter was that he should return to the bosom of the Church, revoke his errors and refrain in future from expressing false teaching and anything that might cause confusion in the Church.

In substance, what was at stake was the teaching of the treasure of the Church. Cajetan based his arguments on the Bull *Unigenitus* of Clement VI, promulgated in 1343. According to this Bull, the pope was permitted to make use of the treasure of the Church that had been acquired through the merits of Christ for the remission of temporal punishment due to sin. Cajetan also rejected the doctrine of the certainty of justification, which Luther believed was required on the basis of the reception of the sacrament, as contradictory both to the teaching of Scripture and to that of the Church. Cajetan instinctively recognised that an affirmation of the certainty of justification pointed clearly in the direction of a new Church. He regarded Luther as someone who could be compared with the conciliarists in that he was opposed to the supreme authority of the pope.

Luther did not believe that he had taught in contradiction to Scripture, the Fathers of the Church, canon law or sound doctrine and regarded his own views as true and Catholic. As a fallible human being, he was ready to submit to the judgment of the legitimate Church and offered himself for public vindication. He could, of course, accept as the voice of Peter only those laws that were in accordance with Scripture and the teaching of the Church Fathers and that was, in his opinion, not so in the case of the Bull *Unigenitus*. According to Paul (Gal. 2), even Peter was able to err, with the result that error could not be excluded in the case of papal laws. He was himself unable to accept that the certainty of justification was a teaching that could simply be set aside. It was a divine truth and even the pope himself was subject to it. Salvation depended on it—his own salvation—and he was prepared to die for it.

Luther's trust in the *papacy* was shaken in the course of his debate with Cajetan. If the pope's power to legislate was not based on the Bible, then not only the Bible, but also the Church were ruined. Luther did not want to cut himself off from the Church in insisting on this. What he rejected, however, was simply an arbitrary form of legislation that was unrelated to Scripture. He therefore turned away from the idea of a badly informed pope to that of a pope who would be better instructed and a little later turned from the pope and appealed to the *conciliar idea*. As human authorities, both could, of course, err, but Luther did not cease to hope that both could make correct decisions on the basis of Scripture. These demands were, however, not in any sense met when the doctrine of indulgences was defined by the pope on 9 November 1548 and he consequently refused to submit to the Church's verdict in the matter of indulgences. He was not, however, at once excommunicated as a rebel, for political reasons.

He wanted to remain in the Church. He believed that his criticism protected the teaching of the Church and that for this reason he did not have to revoke it. At the same time, the conflict with the Church leaders caused him to suffer. He did not take action, but he declared openly in his lectures that necessity might compel obedience of the commandments of the Church, but that one should regard them as worthless. The great number of Church laws was, in his opinion, incompatible with the freedom of the Gospel. He had harsh words to say in this context about the *tyranny of the pope*. For him, the Church was a monarchy of love and service without external power. Because of these views, Luther was at that time quite consciously a 'non-violent' rebel.

(c) The Disputation of Leipzig

The great disputation in Leipzig with Johann Eck that took place in the summer of 1519 seemed to provide a suitable opportunity to settle the disputed theological questions. Eck initiated the debate about *the papacy*. Up till now, he has been regarded as responsible for the drawing up of clear battle lines between the opposing points of view, but it is more true to say that he was very concerned to preserve the unity of the Church.

Luther accepted the need for debate. He wanted to go to the root of the contradictions between the Church's law and the Bible. In the course of his studies of canon law and the history of the Church, he had already begun to suspect that the pope was the Antichrist, 'so wretchedly is Christ, that is, the truth, perverted and crucified by him in the decrees'. The supremacy of pope over the Western (!) Church had, in Luther's opinion, no foundation in the New Testament—it was merely a result of the history of the Church.

Luther was prepared to accept the papacy, at least in so far as it was understood to be an earthly authority and not a supraterrestrial institution. Christ had handed over the office of the keys to the whole Church in the person of Peter and the pope's exclusive claim to it had, in Luther's opinion, led to a Babylonian captivity of the Church and had been the source of the prevailing corruption. The sermon which he preached on Matthew 16 on the feast of Peter and Paul in Leipzig gives a clear indication of the connection that he made between the question of the pope and the doctrine of justification. Luther was only interested in the correct use of the office of the keys as handed over by Christ to all believers, with priests as the ministers of that office. The keys were correctly used as a mediation of grace to the recipient. The all-important factor in this process was, according to Luther, the certainty of grace, through which man might know in his conscience where he was with God.

Eck was triumphant in the disputation about the question of the papacy, especially when he had obliged Luther to declare that some of the statements made by John Huss about the Church and condemned at the Council of Constance were orthodox. These statements came from the Augustinian tradition and Luther was obliged to stand by the position that it would be wrong to allow an article of faith that one recognised to be true to be falsified even by a pope or a council of the Church. Not that he was thereby acting as a presumptuous university professor or theologian who rejected all ecclesiastical authority. At least since he had been condemned by the universities of Louvain and Cologne in 1520, he had known well enough that even professors and university staff could err. The fact that he had to stand alone against the Church and Church authorities gave rise to serious inner misgivings and self-questioning. Nevertheless, as others had learnt before him in the tradition of Christianity, he too knew from Gal. 2 and the history of the Church that it was possible for the truth to be on the side of an individual.

(d) The Decision in Favour of Practical Reform

Strictly speaking, Luther did not cause the revolt against the Church leadership. He saw the problem differently. Power had to be wrested from an insane and tyrannical authority. From 1520 onwards, the Christian rulers seemed to him to have been called to be the only available source of power. He believed that their spiritual authority was derived from the universal priesthood of all believers and that there was no hierarchy in regard to these believers, but only those who ministered to them. When he published his treatise 'inviting the Christian noblemen of the German nation' to 'improve the Christian situation', he hoped to be able to bring about the necessary reform of the Church after the three ways in which the papacy immunised itself—that is, by placing itself above the task of interpreting Scripture, above the activities of the Church's councils and above those of the political powers—had been overcome. Later, he looked forward to the papacy being overcome not by men, but by God himself.

In his *Prelude to the Babylonian Captivity of the Church*, Luther urged the dissociation of the sacraments from human traditions that were clearly not biblical. He sarcastically described this treatise as the first part of the recantation that was once again to be called for in the impending Bull threatening excommunication.

4. THE BREAK WITH ROME

When Luther received the Bull, *Exsurge Domine*, which threatened him with excommunication, at the beginning of October 1520, he made a final attempt at reconciliation in his Letter to Pope Leo X, but, under the existing circumstances and after everything that had been said on both sides, it had little prospect of succeeding. He assured the pope that he respected him and described himself in this letter as a sacrifice to the machinery of the Curia. In a criticism of the Church which he regarded as still necessary, he appealed to the example of Bernard of Clairvaux. He also included with this letter one of his finest treatises, *On the Freedom of a Christian*. This enclosure could certainly not have been accidental. It was clearly intended to serve as an example of how Luther wanted to serve the Church if dissent were permitted in it. Unfortunately, no further dialogue occurred between that Church and its difficult son.

For the rest, all that remained, at first sight at least, was confrontation. Luther declared that the articles that had been rejected in the Bull were necessary to faith. On the basis of his power as a baptised son of God, founded (like Peter!) on the rock, against which the gates of hell could not prevail, he called on the pope and the cardinals to be converted and threatened them too with excommunication. In reaction to the burning of his own books, he burned the Bull of Excommunication on 10 December 1520 and, what was even more incriminating, he also burned the canon law that had made it possible for the Bull to be promulgated. He would very much have liked to have burnt the papal throne itself—'tit for tat'!

This was much more than a reaction of defiance. Although he rejected the Church and its prevailing errors, he wanted to remain in it for the rest of his life. In 1539, he wrote, in his treatise *On Councils and Churches*: 'We are not such desperate people (may God be praised and thanked!) that we have longed for the Church to be ruined, . . . but we are ready to be ruined ourselves until no more flesh or hair remains on us, rather than let harm or suffering befall the Church, in so far as we know or lies within our power.'[2]

Luther's case has many different aspects. Even if we regard the division as inevitable from the very beginning, we are bound to ask whether the Church always dealt in a suitable way with a man who was undoubtedly one of its greatest critics and we are similarly also bound to regret the fact that there was never any real dialogue between him and the Church about what he really wanted to say.

Translated by David Smith

Notes

1. All the material found in this article will be found in Martin Brecht *Luther. Sein Weg zur Reformation 1483-1521* (Stuttgart 1981).
2. See *Martin Luthers Werke. Kritische Gesamtausgabe* 50 (Weimar 1914) p. 516, 24-29.

Gabriel Daly

The Dissent of Theology: The Modernist Crisis

HISTORY, IT has been said, is written by the victors. In a closed, authoritarian, society whose leaders have successfully eliminated significant dissent, history is often indistinguishable from propaganda. The view of 'modernism' which prevailed in the Roman Catholic Church during the half-century which followed its condemnation in 1907 was largely *the product of a skilfully constructed and efficiently disseminated myth*. By using the term 'myth' here I do not intend to imply that the Roman charges against some Catholic scholars in the first decade of the twentieth century were totally without substance, but only that the accusations, based from the start on false premises, were symbolic of an attitude rather than responsive to a real situation.

Throughout the first half of the twentieth century no book or journal bearing an *imprimatur* could with impunity publish conclusions unfavourable to the Roman *magisterium*. This *restriction on scientific freedom and truth* placed Catholic scholars in an impossible situation. Scientific historical research pointed inexorably to conclusions which were discreditable and therefore unacceptable to the Church authorities. In consequence little or no scientific work was done on modernism. Gradually it became permissible to make the timid concession that the authorities had 'overreacted'. Textbooks and encyclopedias, however, continued to propagate the claim made by Pius X's encylical, *Pascendi, dominici gregis*, that modernism was, if not the 'meeting-place of all the heresies', at least a serious attempt to subvert the Church doctrinally and philosophically, and that the modernists were a united and sinister faction intent upon the destroying from within the very foundations of Catholic faith. The ordinary *magisterium* of the Church had stated that there was such a conspiracy and moreover had gone on to specify its main theological characteristics. Whatever might be thought in private, there could be no public challenge to one of the most successful myths ever released into the Catholic Church.

1. PASCENDI DOMINICI GREGIS

What, then, did *Pius X* and his senior advisers have in mind when they spoke of 'modernism'? What they said they had in mind is contained in Pius's encyclical *Pascendi*. The 'theoretical' part of the document is a fascinating exercise in theological make-believe. Before our eyes the author, Joseph Lemius, conjures up a system of thought which no theologian, Catholic or Protestant, had ever held.

Pascendi comprises a pastiche of ideas assembled mainly from the writings of Alfred Loisy and Auguste Sabatier and deployed without nuance in a manner which suggests that it constitutes its own refutation (there is hardly any speculative refutation in the encyclical). To anyone unfamiliar with the originals which it caricatures it must have been largely incomprehensible. Doubtless many a seminary professor scratched his head over it and turned with premature relief to the 'disciplinary' portion. Here, amid the most ferocious assembly of anti-liberal and anti-intellectual measures ever devised by a Church authority, lay two phrases which struck at the heart, not just of academic freedom, but of basic human rights: 'Anyone found to be tainted with modernism (*modo quopiam modernismo imbuti*) is to be excluded without compunction from the offices both of government and of teaching.'[1] Bishops are exhorted to do all in their power to suppress writings which 'smack of modernism' (*quae modernismum olent*).

To make these measures effective the Church is to be policed by 'vigilance committees' in every diocese.[2] To be delated was, in principle, to be found guilty. There was no trial, no facing of one's accuser—delators were guaranteed anonymity—no possibility of making a defence, and, of course, no appeal against sentence. Long after the paranoia had subsided, the myth of a concerted heretical campaign within the Church lingered on, reinforced by the anti-modernist oath prescribed in 1910.

2. TOWARDS A DEFINITION

It is important to realise that *Pascendi* not merely condemned modernism: it defined it; and the definition has proved to be more durable than the condemnation. There are contemporary Catholic theologians who appear still to hold the view that although the Roman response to 'modernism' was indefensibly violent and hyperbolic, there was nevertheless some sort of dangerous movement afoot. To describe modernism as 'a movement', even without the epithet 'heretical', implies acceptance of *Pascendi's* principal, and least critically acceptable, contention. The encyclical chose to interpret a scattering of non-scholastic scholars as a concerted movement. The only movement afoot in the Church at that time was the movement which crushed all dissent from Ultramontane scholasticism. It is precisely because modernism was *not* a movement that Rome was able to destroy, as 'modernist', all manifestation of liberal thought so easily. There are therefore good *theological* reasons for abandoning the term 'modernism' altogether; but this is not *historically* feasible, if only because its use, inaccurate and tendentious though it was, is a fact of history.

If we continue to use the term, we must take the greatest care to define it in the light of critical research. The definition should, I submit, be framed in such a way as (*a*) to recognise that the Roman condemnation is a major element in the data (in short, it is part of the overall problem); (*b*) to allow modernism to be related to, though distinguished from, the 'Reform-Catholicism' that preceded it and the 'New Theology' that followed it in the 1940s; (*c*) to make it unnecessary for anxious admirers of men like Blondel and von Hügel to have to prove that their man was 'not a modernist'; and (*d*) to leave open questions concerning the orthodoxy of any individual modernist.

Accordingly I put forward the following: 'Modernism' was the term employed by Pius X and his senior curial advisers in their attempt to describe and condemn certain liberal, anti-scholastic, and historico-critical forms of thought occurring in the Roman Catholic Church between *c.* 1890 and 1910.

Each of the men who came to be regarded as leaders of the alleged movement, together with their sympathisers, was conscious of sharing loosely in an intra-mural dissent from certain cultural features of the prevailing Catholic theology of their age. Leaving aside disciplinary and legal questions and restricting one's attention to the purely theological, one can instance four such features from which the modernists dissented.

(a) Mandatory Thomism

We are dealing here not with Thomism as one of the great schools of Catholic theology, but with neo-Thomism as a philosophico-theological system *imposed* upon the Church by papal command. It is easy to underrate the significance of *Leo XIII*'s encyclical, *Aeterni Patris* (of which the centenary passed in 1979 with little or no comment), and the administrative steps the pope took to ensure that his grand design should be effectively executed.

George Tyrrell described this move as 'Medievalism', i.e., an attempt to recreate the intellectual climate of the thirteenth century as a means of protecting nineteenth-century Catholic faith from the challenges of modernity. Loisy informed Harnack that the Catholic Church 'is bound to the science and political form of the middle ages only because it does not choose to detach itself from them'.[3] The anti-modernist campaign and its eventual success reinforced the thrust of Leo's programme and bound it more firmly to the prevailing concept of Catholic orthodoxy. *Pascendi* declared Catholic orthodoxy to be inseparable from its scholastic expression: '. . . there is no surer sign that a man is tending to modernism than when he begins to show his dislike for the scholastic method.'[4] *Humani Generis* (1950) was to say much the same thing, though in gentler language, about the 'New Theology'.

(b) Integralism

'Integralism' was the term employed by defenders of the view that Catholic orthodoxy is expressed in, and inextricably bound up with, a logically organised system of inter-connected doctrines each of which goes to make up a divinely guaranteed whole. Joseph Lemius expressed the integralist view in an unpublished lecture he gave to the Academy of St Thomas in Rome in 1907, only a few months before he was commissioned to draft the 'theoretical' portion of *Pascendi*.

'In a system of doctrines so rigorously connected and linked as is the system of Aristotle and the Angelic Doctor, no single point can be detached from the others, [since] the light of truth which illumines each individual part is the same as that which illumines the whole.'[5]

Integralism sought a similar structural cohesion in the positions it wished to attack. This type of systematic cohesion belongs in the main to deductive thought, whereas the modernists were dealing in induction based on history (Loisy), experience (Tyrrell and von Hügel), or the analysis of human dynamic (Blondel and Laberthonnière). The theoretical portion of *Pascendi* shows us the integralist mind in the act of creating a counter-system in its own image and likeness.

The integralists lumped their opponents together and condemned them indiscriminately. Thus Louis Billot's book, *De immutabilitate traditionis contra modernam haeresim evolutionismi*,[6] treats Laberthonnière with greater hostility than it does Loisy. The absurdity of this attitude was largely due to Billot's detestation of Blondel's 'Method of Immanence' which rejected the deductive method that Billot believed to be essential to the deployment and defence of Catholic truth.

(c) Biblical and Dogmatic Fundamentalism

In the words of Karl Barth, Kant had offered 'terms of peace' to theology. Liberal

Protestantism did what it could with those terms, while *neo-scholastic Catholicism persisted in denying that there was a case to answer*, much less a peace to be negotiated. The modernists appreciated the fact that there was a case to answer and that, as Blondel put it, Aristotle was not the man to do the answering. Blondel therefore saw himself as trying 'to accomplish for the Catholic form of religious thought what Germany has done long ago and continues to do for the Protestant form. . . .'[7] Any effective form of Catholic apologetic would have to accept human religious experience as its starting point. This conviction constituted the philosophical foundation of modernism, and it was rejected out of hand by the integralists as 'Kantian subjectivism'.

The *biblical* scholars of the period had to face the prevailing *fundamentalism* which was indispensable to the historical links in the integralist chain. Billot viewed any appeal to critical history as dogmatic treason. Biblical study therefore became, in Loisy's phrase, 'like tight-rope walking'.[8] Apart from Loisy, the biblical modernists were discreet and self-effacing. The trials and tribulations of Lagrange and Genocchi vividly illustrate the difficulties of their task. *Providentissimus Deus* had encouraged biblical study, but whenever the findings of this study seemed to conflict with any part of the *a prioristic* dogmatic system, they were condemned as erroneous or dangerous.

(*d*) Ultramontanism

The anti-modernist campaign would have been impossible without the papal centralism which was the immediate result of the First Vatican Council. The bishops of the Church accepted without demur the diagnosis given, and the remedy prescribed, by *Pascendi* and *Sacrorum antistitum*. If many of them failed to implement all the measures prescribed by the encyclical, this was simply because they saw no evidence of modernism in their dioceses—which is an illuminating comment on the state of Catholic theology at the time.

On the whole the modernists did not parade their dissent but did all they could to maintain their ecclesial links intact. Von Hügel even proclaimed that he was an Ultramontane of the *old*, pre-Vatican I, school ('Ultramontane' here meaning little more than anti-Erastian). In their private correspondence the modernists expressed voluble dissent from latter-day Ultramontanism, but only Tyrrell and the Roman modernists gave full and public utterance to these views. Tyrell did so, under extreme pressure, in his book *Medievalism*.[9]

This book was occasioned by the fact that Cardinal Mercier of Malines had taken the extraordinary step of mentioning Tyrrell by name in his Lenten Pastoral for 1908. *Medievalism* is unique among modernist writings. It throws ecclesiastical caution to the winds, yet it observes all the decencies of debate. It is written in a prose which is taut, limpid, and vigorous. There are few clearer statements of the case against Ultramontanism. It is also a distillation of Tyrrell's views on what the modernists were struggling to bring about.

> 'Let us, then, keep the word "Modernist" to designate those who believe in the Roman Catholic Church as firmly as medievalists do; but whose deeper faith is not frightened but stimulated by the assured results of modern criticism.'[10]

This is surely a worthy statement of theological purpose even today. Tyrrell goes on to speak of his 'dream':

> '. . . when the Catholic people represented by their bishops and their pope will assemble, not to decide and impose points of theology, ethics and politics "under pain of eternal damnation", but to proclaim the Gospel of God's Kingdom upon

earth as it was proclaimed by Jesus Christ; to preach "unity in essentials, liberty in non-essentials, charity in all things".[11]

The *Second Vatican Council* went far towards meeting the major lineaments of Tyrrell's dream, though he would, I suspect, have been dismayed to discover how deep the roots of Ultramontanism had reached and how easily they could be made to germinate anew in a populist atmosphere when the will to collegiality appears, temporarily at least, to have weakened.

Notes

1. *Acta Apostolicae Sedis* 40 (1907) p. 642.
2. *Ibid*. p. 647.
3. A. Loisy *L'Évangile et L'Église* (Paris 1902) p. 34.
4. *Acta Apostolicae Sedis* 40 (1907) pp. 636-637.
5. Cited, with Italian original, in G. Daly *Transcendence and Immanence: A Study in Catholic Modernism and Integralism* (Oxford 1980) p. 184 and footnote.
6. Rome 1907.
7. M. Blondel *Lettres philosophiques* (Paris 1961) p. 34.
8. A. Loisy *Autour d'un petit livre* (Paris 1903) p. 218.
9. G. Tyrrell *Medievalism: A Reply to Cardinal Mercier* (London 1908).
10. Tyrrell *Medievalism* p. 145.
11. *Ibid*. p. 187.

PART IV

Biblical Norms

Roland E. Murphy

Prophets and Wise Men as Provokers of Dissent

1. PROPHETS AS PROTESTERS IN THE NAME OF THE LORD

THE POPULAR image of a biblical prophet is that of a protester in the name of the Lord. One need only recall the scene on Mt. Carmel, where Elijah challenges the people to follow the Lord (1 Kings 18:21), the confrontation which Amos has with Amaziah the priest at the royal temple in Bethel (Amos 7:10-17), Jeremiah's being placed in the stocks (Jer. 20:1-6) and finally in prison (Jer. 37-38). It was an appropriate title for any prophet that king Ahab gave to Elijah: 'you disturber of Israel!' (1 Kings 18:17). The prophets provoked opposition by their preaching: opposition from the State, from institutionalised religion, from the *vox populi*, and perhaps the most searing experience of all, from other prophets.

(a) Mandate and Message

The mandate for such a disturbing mission is a simple one: a *commission from the Lord*. Most of the prophets are unwilling to accept the call; Jeremiah pleads that he is too young (Jer. 1:6); Amos surely did not seek it when he was taken 'from following the flock' and told to go to the people of Israel (Amos 7:15). Only Isaiah responded spontaneously to the imperious question, 'Who shall go for us?' (Isa. 6:8). However, the clarity with which the mandate is expressed should not deceive us. It did not guarantee inner certainty, nor did it deliver the protection and support which it seemed to promise. *Jeremiah* is told:

> But do you gird up your loins;
>   stand up and tell them
>   all that I command you. . . .
> They will fight against you, but not prevail over you,
>   for I am with you to deliver you, says the Lord (Jer. 1:17-19).

But it is Jeremiah himself who describes his commission in realistic terms:

You duped me, O Lord, and I let myself be duped;
   you were too strong for me, and you triumphed. . . .
The word of the Lord has brought me
   derision and reproach, all the day (Jer. 20:7-8).

Despite the impressive credentials that the prophet might display, despite the exalted nature of the calling, he usually paid a price. It is not inappropriate to recall here the words Jesus addressed to Jerusalem: 'murderers of prophets and stoner of those who were sent to you' (Matt. 23:37). No one who would be a 'twentieth-century prophet' should be unaware of the risks involved.[1]

What is *the message* of dissent that is formulated by the prophets? It varies according to changing political and social situations. *Elijah* takes a position against the growing worship of Baal which threatens to unseat the religion of Yahweh. *Amos* is against the social injustices (5:9-15), which afflict the poor, contrary to the covenant agreement, and against the formality of religious sacrifice which makes possible a 'cover-up' among the mainstream worshippers (Amos 5:21, 'I hate, I spurn your feasts'). *Jeremiah* attacks the false security which derived from the presence of the Lord among his people: the temple of the Lord (Jer. 7:4). This issue illustrates the importance of heeding the particular concrete historical situations in which the prophet lived.

About a hundred years before Jeremiah, *Isaiah* of Jerusalem preaches the inviolability, the invincibility of Zion (14:32; 29:8; 31:1-9; see Pss. 46, 48). This is not to say that Isaiah did not also preach a hard line, and also threaten destruction (1:21-31; 3:1-4:1). His contemporary, *Micah*, was remembered a hundred years later as having announced the demolition of the temple (Jer. 26:18), and this is an important factor in Jeremiah's deliverance from death.

But the fact that Isaiah took a strong stand on the inviolability of Jerusalem against the invasions of Assyria, especially when Sennacherib's army stood outside the gates of Jerusalem (Is. 36-37), made it possible for an overweening pride and a dangerous certainty to take over when the power of Babylon was threatening in the time of Jeremiah (597, the first siege and wave of exiles; 587, the destruction of Jerusalem). It is an example of how the proper message in one age can become a draught of poison for another generation. The specific circumstances have to be recalled lest the message itself become a trap. A selective hearing of the prophetical message can lead to destruction.

(b) The Struggle about Israel's Election

A more central and dramatic instance of dissent than that of *Amos* can hardly be imagined. He personally dissented from, and urged the people to dissent from a basic element of Israelite faith: *election*.

Are you not like the Ethiopians to me,
   O men of Israel, says the Lord?
Did I not bring the Israelites from the land of Egypt
   As I brought the Philistines from Caphtor
   and the Arameans from Kir? (Amos 9:7).

Amos believed in the tradition that the Lord had elected Israel; indeed he brought them 'from the land of Egypt'. But Israel had come to conceive this as an unconditional, fixed, belief that guaranteed her existence, and ultimately put her in a privileged status *vis-à-vis* other peoples. It was all very consoling to recite the 'Israelite creed' of Deuteronomy 26:5-10. The doctrine of salvation history seemed to lock the people into the Lord's perpetual concern; he would always come to the rescue. This understanding was common, and they looked forward to the 'day of the Lord', when he would intervene in their favour. But, said Amos, it will be a day of 'darkness, not light!' (Amos 5:18-20). The history of salvation has become the 'history of decision'.[2]

One prophet, *Habakkuk*, dares to question the Lord directly concerning the divine plans. Roughly contemporary with Jeremiah (*c.* 605), he is unwilling to accept the Babylonians (the 'Chaldeans') as the proper means to correct Israel's infidelity. Can the Lord look on 'while the wicked man devours one more just than himself' (1:13). He takes up a post to see what the Lord will answer to his complaint, and he received the mysterious answer.

> *The rash man has no integrity,*
>   *but the just man, because of his faith, shall live*
>   *(Hab. 2:4).*

This is a hard answer, because it provides no easy way out; one has to persevere and not give up. It is the same kind of answer that *Jeremiah* received when he complained about the treatment he received from his opponents, among whom were his own relatives who sought to kill him: 'If running against men has wearied you, how will you race against horses?' (Jer. 12:5). It is the integrity of the *prophet's life* that was probably the best *sign of his credibility*.

Not many prophets were successful in their own generation. Isaiah was forced to gather a loyal group of followers around him (Isa. 8:16). Jeremiah was accused of being a traitor (Jer. 38:4) and was eventually coerced by his own people into fleeing into exile in Egypt. Indeed, the man becomes the message. In the case of Jeremiah one can see a *change of focus from the message to the person of the prophet*. His word still remains important, but his life is equally so; hence the biography of Jeremiah by Baruch (Jer. 37-45). The prophets were not interested in building any power base. It is true that Jeremiah receives some protection from the family of Shaphan which has some power in the court (Jer. 36), but political manoeuvering is not the prophetic style. They knew how unstable it was to 'trust in princes' (Pss. 118:99; 146:3).

(c) The Criteria for True Prophecy

The above contrast between Isaiah and Jeremiah alerts us to the concreteness and specificity of the prophetic word. Dissent was more of a *practical* than a theoretical nature; in general praxis prevails over theology in Israelite thought. The Lord alone was to be worshipped, and this 'great commandment' (Deut. 5:6-7), along with covenant stipulations, formed the test of Israel's faith. It is almost uncanny how the prophets refuse to be caught up in popular religion which would attempt to placate the Lord by selective sacrifices, while the weightier matters of the Law went unobserved. Political issues were not decided from the point of view of politics or the civil welfare of the State. King Ahaz cannot believe in the assurances of the prophet Isaiah, so he calls upon the help of Tiglathpileser of Assyria in order to secure victory over the Syrians and the northern kingdom of Israel. Jeremiah preaches submission to the Babylonians as the will of the Lord (Jer. 27-29), a manifestly unpopular stand which is judged to be traitorous. The agony of it all is that not just the leaders, but the people remain unresponsive. The prophets were failures in their generation, yet 'successful failures' in the light of later generations which were responsible for the transmission and eventual canonisation of their writings.

In their own lifetime they were confronted by those who are too conveniently termed 'false prophets' today. Jeremiah and Ezekiel in particular have sharp words for such prophets, and they brand them as false (Jer. 23:9-40; Ezek. 13). But this should not blind us to the complexity of the situation. What criteria were applied to the prophets? Deuteronomy (13:2-6 and 18:21-22) lays down some tests: *orthodoxy* of message, and *fulfilment* of the prophetic word. But these tests seem to have been more retroactive than functional in the lives of the prophets themselves.

Jeremiah, in his famous altercation with the prophet Hananiah (Jer. 28:5-9) invokes the argument of burden of proof against him: if you are going to prophecy peace, some sign of fulfilment is necessary. One learns from such a conflict as this of the uncertainty with which a genuine prophet could be afflicted. Jeremíah does 'put down' Hananiah when the latter with great panache breaks the symbolic yoke from the neck of the prophet to indicate that thus the power of the Babylonians shall be broken by the Lord in Israel's favour. Now Jeremiah departs, with nothing to say in reply. There can be no question but that he was assailed with doubts. Was it possible that the Lord had changed his message, that he was now speaking a consoling word through another prophet, Hananiah? The laconic text reads: 'At that the prophet Jeremiah went away. Some time after the prophet Hananiah had broken the yoke off the neck of the prophet Jeremiah, the word of the Lord came to Jeremiah . . .' (Jer. 28:11-12). The agony of Jeremiah in the meantime must have been devastating.

2. THE DISSENT OF THE WISE MEN

The biblical prophets present a vivid picture of dissent in the name of the Lord. Not as vivid, but no less significant in the *dissent* that emerges in the wisdom literature, such as Job, Ecclesiastes, and some of the Psalms, *against the reigning theory of divine justice*. The type of dissent voiced in this literature appears to be theoretical and theological, but it grew out of bitter experience.

The doctrine of the Israelite wise men, as this is reflected in *the book of Proverbs*, insists that wisdom leads to success and prosperity, while folly brings destruction. The perspective is, of course, limited to this life, and both wisdom and folly are practical conduct, not just theoretical knowledge. But the doctrine is basically optimistic in its theory of retribution. The wisdom teachers are not alone in this. They share in the common doctrine of the Bible that *God rewards the good and punishes the evil*. In the stirring words of Moses in Deut. 30:15ff., there was a choice of life, if one obeyed the directives of God, or of death, if one disobeyed. The three friends who dialogue with Job carry the doctrine to its ultimate conclusion: Job must have done something wrong, since the divine justice is indisputable.

The author of *the book of Job* writes one of the largest pages of dissent in the Bible when he sets out to *contradict* this basic datum of *Israel's understanding of existence*. He does not see clearly enough to replace the reigning view with another one. But he succeeds in displacing it from its dominant position, and to provide an opening into the mystery of God's dealings with human beings. As the poet Robert Frost conceives it in 'The Masque of Reason', God is able to thank Job for having set him free to reign, and not be bound by human standards of justice. In Job this dissent is played out against the emotional background of a suffering man who struggles with the lectures which his friends deliver to him, but most of all with the God whom he cannot understand.

The book of Ecclesiastes, or *Qohelet*, is less passionate, but even more devastating. He has an eye for the injustice that Job takes account of: 'the sinner does evil a hundred times and survives' (Eccles. 8:12); 'love from hatred man cannot tell, both appear equally vain' (9:1).

In the cold light of Qohelet's analysis, there is nothing in our experience that shows whether God loves a person, or hates him. This is because 'among all things that happen under the sun, this is the worst, that things turn out the same for all' (9:3). Qohelet clearly claims that *humans cannot make out what God is doing*: 'So you know not the work of God which he is accomplishing in the universe' (11:5; see 8:17). He does not deny that God is master and sovereign of all that happens; on the contrary, this truth is at the basis of his claims. He denies that one can make any sense of what God is doing. Neither does he deny that God is a judge. But this is an inert truth; one knows nothing about the judgment of God. For all this, Qohelet does not raise the banner of revolution. He dissents from a comfortable understanding of divine retribution, but without giving up faith.

It is not easy for us to picture the circumstances in which the books of Job and Ecclesiastes were received. We do know that at the time of *Rabbi Akiba* (died *c.* A.D. 135) there was doubt about the canonicity of Ecclesiastes. Obviously some found his dissent more than they could tolerate. Perhaps the most perplexing factor is that Qohelet never took an open position on the traditional themes of salvation history (which are highly interpretive of God's designs). He stayed severely within the framework of wisdom: the realm of experience.

In *Jesus Christ* we come to one who was both prophet and sage, one who was commissioned to preach the *Kingdom*, and one who spoke about it in parables drawn from human experience. In this dual role he lived up to, and even surpassed, his predecessors along the path of dissent in which they had walked. It is interesting to observe that there is no significant dissent on the doctrine of a future life. Rather he emphasised the *quality* of this life. He clashed with the position of the Sadducees concerning the next life (Matt. 22:22ff.), but there were weightier matters of dissent: the concrete actions of daily living, such as we find in the so-called 'antitheses' of the Sermon on the Mount. A central point is the teaching on love:

> You have heard the commandment, 'You shall love your countryman but hate your enemy'. My command to you is: love your enemies, pray for your persecutors. This will prove that you are sons of your Father, for his sun rises on the bad and the good, he rains on the just and the unjust. If you love those who love you, what merit is there in that? Do not tax collectors do as much? And if you greet your brothers only, what is so praiseworthy about that? Do not pagans do as much? In a word, you must be made perfect as your heavenly Father is perfect (Matt. 5:43-48).

The 'commandment' Jesus refers to is really not present in the Old Testament. The reference seems to be to Lev. 19:18, but the words 'hate your enemy' are absent. Jesus is not setting aside an Old Testament belief; he is attacking a particular understanding of it. Equivalently he is saying: *'this is your understanding of the Law, but I tell you. . . .'* He dissents from a regnant interpretation of the Law in order to present his own view. He is striking out against a mentality which was obviously current in his day. This attitude can be exemplified from the sectarian rule of the Essene community found among the so-called Dead Sea Scrolls (1QS, or *Serek*, 1:7ff.). It is not that he is in direct dialogue with the Essenes; he is combatting a mentality which their teaching exemplified.

This dissent might be considered purely theoretical, were it not for the very life of Jesus. As with Jeremiah, the man became the message. The nature of love of neighbour is *revealed* in the life of Jesus himself, his unlimited giving of himself, even unto death. Hence the early Church could define love of God in terms of the life of Jesus (1 John 4:7-12). Paul, as W. D. Davies puts it, 'urges us not so much to love our neighbour and to love God as to look at Jesus and then to love our neighbour in his light'.[3]

Jesus was not an iconoclast. Rather he was truly a 'radical'. He radicalised love by his death; he radicalised dissent by his life.

Notes

1. See W. S. Towner 'On Calling People "Prophets" in 1970' *Interpretation* 24 (1970) 492-509.
2. This is the view of John J. Collins in his perceptive article 'History and Tradition in the Prophet Amos' *Irish Theological Quarterly* 41 (1974) 120-133.
3. See W. D. Davies *The Setting of the Sermon on the Mount* (Cambridge University Press 1964) p. 407.

Hermann-Josef Venetz

Dealing with Dissenters in the New Testament Communities

1. 'DISSENTERS' AND 'THOSE IN A POSITION OF RESPONSIBILITY'

THE NEW TESTAMENT does not provide any immediate access to those who opposed its authors. Dissenters do of course crop up in their writings, and the purpose of this essay is to investigate how they dealt with them. The historical question about these dissenters—their significance, their intentions, the nature of their opposition, their relationship to the Christian community, etc.—can therefore only be answered within the framework of the literary question of the texts available to us.

Often enough the New Testament writers do not engage directly in controversy with these dissenters. They address communities and individuals in order to inform them about these dissenters and/or to give them advice about how they for their part should deal with them. Hence dissenters occur more frequently in the third than in the second person in the writings of the New Testament.

Within the framework of this indirect approach there is considerable variation in the way in which dissenters crop up in the New Testament writings: they are quoted directly (1 Cor. 15:12),[1] they are identified as different groups in the gospels ('the disciples', 'the pharisees', 'the Jews', 'the multitude', etc.), their arguments are put in the mouth of an imagined interlocutor (Rom. 2), they appear as enemies conceived of in mythical terms (Revelation), as 'anti-Christs' (1 John), etc. They do not have any opportunity of commenting on the views ascribed to them, which may be understood correctly or misunderstood, or of replying to accusations, traducements and distortions.

It is not without significance to observe that the New Testament writings that engaged in arguments with dissenters were written by people who were in a *position of responsibility* with regard to their audience (opponents, communities, groups, individuals). For the sake of simplicity we shall call them people in a position of responsibility without thereby ascribing to them the responsibility of community leaders or refusing their opponents all responsibility, including responsibility within the Church. What is important is to keep as clearly as possible before one's eyes the situation in which these arguments took place: something that is not always easy, since it can only occasionally be deduced from the texts with sufficient certainty.

It is not every form of sinful behaviour or behaviour that departs from that of the majority or from a definite norm that is thereby an example of dissent (e.g., the story of

Ananias and Sapphira in Acts 5:1-11), and it is not every dogmatic statement in the New Testament that should be interpreted as a reply to opposition (e.g., the beatitudes). In this essay we shall classify as dissenters those who as a matter of considered policy adopt a deviant position and in certain circumstances cling to it.[2]

2. FACTORS THAT DETERMINE HOW DISSIDENTS ARE DEALT WITH

For dealing with dissidents in our age there are no normative rules that can immediately be derived from the New Testament.[3] One would need to initiate an investigation that would embrace all the cases in the New Testament in which the traces of dispute with dissidents are more or less clear. In this perhaps quite definite principles would become clear which could claim to be normative for a later age. But this kind of investigation could not be carried out in the scanty space available.

What is proposed here is a different, less pretentious approach which, it is hoped, will lead to solutions being at least indicated. It is a question of keeping one's eye on those factors that decisively influence the way dissidents are dealt with. We are induced to adopt this procedure by a series of studies which have as their object the *difference in the treatment of heretics as between the genuine Pauline writings and the pastoral epistles*.[4] The results of these investigations should also be of significance in dealing with other New Testament writings.

The list that follows is not meant to be exhaustive, and if it is not possible to throw enough exegetical light on each of the factors the reason is the lack of space.

(a) Personal presuppositions

Without depending on particular texts it needs to be suggested that a certain role is played by the *temperament* of the person in a position of responsibility in determining the kind of way in which dissenters are dealt with. Typical here would be Paul, with his temperament marked by considerable swings of mood. It can indeed be established that he gave freer rein to his temperament when dealing with communities that he knew well (1 Cor. 4:21; Phil. 3:2).

But even in the case of the synoptics and the tradition they were drawing on temperament should not be left completely out of account. For example, if the discussion about which is the first or greatest commandment takes on one occasion the form of a dialogue between teacher and pupil (Mark 12:28-34), on a second occasion the form of a polemical disputation (Matt. 22:34-40), and on the third occasion a stronger exhortatory form (Luke 10:25-37), whatever stage in the development of the tradition these may represent, then this has clearly something to do with the author's temperament among other factors.

The way dissenters are dealt with is influenced by the *outlook* of the person concerned. Various writings and passages of the New Testament display an apocalyptic or dualistic view of the world. This naturally does not give dissenters much time and has little need for shades of meaning to characterise them beyond black and white. Dissenters are identified with the 'scoffers' who 'will come in the last days' (2 Peter 3:3), with 'false Christs and false prophets' (Mark 13:22). They are described in mythical terms as those that have the devil as their father (John 8:44), as those who worship the dragon and the beast (Rev. 13:4). Writers in the wisdom tradition may mark themselves off more sharply from dissidents but will be more open towards other experiences and insights and will make the effort to carry conviction and appear reasonable. We should mention the synoptics' treatment of the sayings of Jesus,[5] the letter to the Ephesians composed as a discourse on wisdom,[6] or James's combination of exhortation and teaching.[7] Included in this outlook should also be that which sees things in terms of the history of salvation, as for example is found in the basic outline of Luke's writings, in the speeches in the Acts of the Apostles, in the allegorical treatment of the parables (particularly in Matthew), and in the 'treatise on the Jews' (Romans 9-11).[8]

The *literary and rhetorical gifts* of the person in a position of responsibility or of the author should also be regarded as a significant factor that determines the way dissidents are tackled. It is interesting that those disputes that are influenced by Jesus (in the gospels) display a great wealth of literary ideas. Here we find predominantly narrative elements like parables and exemplary tales, but also a variety of argumentative forms like comparisons, analogies, proverbs, counter-questions, etc. Paul, too, has at his disposal a rich palette of argumentative devices, and he seems to have been well at home in the rhetorical skills of the ancient world.[9] Other writings hardly vary their argumentative techniques (1 John) or are content with denial and putting right or even refrain from any argument at all (the pastoral epistles, Jude, 2 Peter).

A decisive effect on the way in which dissidents are handled is exercised by the *theological competence and creativity* of the person concerned—qualities shown above all by Paul. The independence, keenness and creativity of his theological ability aided him in dealing with dissidents when he continually thought up new arguments to use against them. He drew them from the primitive Christian creed, from the Old Testament, from experience, from philosophy, from psychology, from cosmology, etc. (see 1 Cor. 9 and 15, Galatians, Romans).[10]

In contrast hardly an original theological argument is to be found in the pastoral epistles. The style of argument is hidebound and is often content with referring to 'good doctrine' and 'sound words' (1 Tim. 4:6, 6:3; 2 Tim. 2:14; Titus 3:8). Dissenters are disqualified on moral grounds (1 Tim. 1:7, 4:2, 6:4-5): it is not erroneous doctrines but those who propound them that are attacked.[11]

Not without importance is the *understanding of faith* or concept of truth held by the person concerned in dealings with dissenters. While for the synoptics faith is interpreted more in the sense of trust 'that changes can take place in apparently unchangeable aspects of the world',[12] according to Paul faith is the 'acceptance in trust of the fate of Christ', to which corresponds 'a new and, with regard to the law, different attitude of the believer towards himself or herself and towards the world and a new pattern of behaviour that finds its criteria in that'.[13]

The understanding of faith shown by the pastoral epistles, Jude and 2 Peter is considerably different. Admittedly, in these writings faith also means personal belief (2 Peter 1:5),[14] and the normative concepts of deposit and teaching do not simply qualify faith as doctrine.[15] But to a greater extent faith is a 'pious family heirloom'[16] that has been delivered once and for all (Jude 3): in it truth is present and in a certain sense also available (2 Peter 1:12). From the point of view of the believer it was presented to him or her 'in the form of the fulfilment of a series of virtues'.[17]

A further factor affecting the way dissidents are dealt with is the *intensity of the relationship* between the person concerned and the congregation or individuals he is addressing. The observation that the epistle to the Galatians has a more polemical tone than that to the Romans is as old as the letters themselves. That to the Galatians is of course more 'topical' than that to the Romans. But it should be correct to observe that writings which do not seem to have a specific audience are more restrained and general in tone when it comes to polemics (Ephesians, James, 1 Peter).

This can be put the other way by noting that, if there is a great distance between the author and the community or dissenters he is dealing with or if he does not know them, there is a danger of the dissenters being generalised and distorted. This danger can at least be surmised in Jude and 2 Peter. In Revelation downright mythical traits are applied to the inaccessible dissidents and those who side with them (Rev. 13).

A certain significance attaches to the way in which the person in a position of responsibility *assesses the form that dissent takes*. Does dissent arise from an existential concern (1 Thess. 4:13-18), a pastoral concern (1 Cor. 7:1-24), a dogmatic concern (1 Cor. 15:1-58), or from an antinomian concern (1 Cor. 6:12-20)? Does it call into question the existence of the person responsible as an apostle (1 Cor. 9; 2 Cor. 10:12-12:13)? Does it threaten his laborious missionary work (Galatians; Phil. 3:1-11)? Is it likely to split the community (1 Cor. 1:10-13) or to isolate the person in a position of responsibility (Gal. 1-2)? With Paul the origin and type of dissent are assessed differently and as a result his opponents are dealt with in very different ways. But in the pastoral epistles there is hardly any trace of this kind of nuanced treatment.[18] There is thus a uniform tone in their dealings with dissenters, a tone that is uniformly polemical and moralising.

(b) The effect of the situation

Significant for dealing with dissidents is the way the person in a position of responsibility *understands his role or office*. Paul's 'role' with regard to the various communities he is in contact with cannot be defined without further investigation. He sees himself as the founder of the Christian community and a missionary, compares himself to a father and presents himself as an example (1 Cor. 3:5-11, 4:14-17, Romans 15:20). He relies on his personal qualities rather than pulling rank, as is especially well shown by his passionate appeals in 2 Corinthians. A different picture is presented by the pastoral epistles. What predominates in them is the 'principle of office'.[19] Even if a more precise title for Timothy and Titus cannot be agreed upon, there is no doubt about the way they understand themselves as leaders of the community, nor about the way the author of these letters sees himself. This is indeed an additional reason for treating dissenters in such a decisive, not to say outspoken, way. In addition we should notice the almost 'complete retreat of the community': it has become a 'praying and listening community'. 'Prophets' and 'teachers' in the sense of the earlier epistles are excluded.[20] As authentic guardians of the deposit of faith and thus to a certain extent the ultimate tribunal for their opponents, Timothy and Titus (as indeed the author of the pastoral epistles himself) bring their office, and hardly ever themselves, into play.

A discussion with dissidents can be conducted on the basis of the facts or by appeal to an external authority. Paul, for whom the entire community (including his opponents?) is 'the body of Christ' (see 1 Cor. 12), only rarely appeals to the authority of Jesus (1 Cor. 7:10, 9:14).

The appeal to the authority of Jesus takes place quite differently in Matthew, namely, in terms of details of the narrative within the larger framework of the literary genre of 'gospel'. But even here an inadmissible appeal to the authority of Jesus is recognised and rejected (Matt. 7:22-23, see Luke 13:26-27). The Jesus of the Fourth Gospel clearly speaks the language of its author.

In the pseudepigraphical writings the authors in their different ways appeal to an undisputed authority. While the claim of Colossians and Ephesians (assuming them not to be authentic) has internal cohesion in the sense of a genuine continuation of Pauline theology, the pastoral epistles' appeal to Paul is almost entirely external. Pauline theology can hardly be discovered in the pastoral epistles: their final and only authority is 'Paul' as their ostensible author.

The way dissenters are dealt with depends on *the way members of the community are evaluated* by the person in a position of responsibility. Although Paul can have his doubts about the maturity of his audience (1 Cor. 3:1-2), he is nevertheless ready to expect something of them, and this morally as well as intellectually. This is shown by the way he invites communities to endure conflicts (compare the 'strong' and the 'weak' in

Corinth and Rome: 1 Cor. 8, Romans 14), or by the way he provides them with arguments to help them make up their minds (1 Cor. 7), or by the way he expects them to conduct a theologically responsible dispute themselves with the opponents (2 Cor. 5:12, see also Col. 2:4, 16-23).

The author of the pastoral epistles does not have much confidence in the communities: he is worried about the moral decay caused by 'evil' dissenters and recommends avoiding superfluous discussion and keeping one's distance from them (1 Tim. 6:20; 2 Tim. 2:23-24, 4:15; Titus 3:9).

The way dissenters are dealt with depends on the way the person in a position of responsibility *understands the Christian community*. This is not something that is the same in all the writings of the New Testament.[21] For example, we can compare 1 Cor. 12, where a more co-operative understanding of the community is expressed through the image of the body and its members, with the pastoral epistles, Jude and 2 Peter, where increasingly an authoritarian understanding of the community is brought to bear and the authors reach pretty authoritarian decisions. In Acts 15 the 'dissension' that broke out at Antioch is decided by the 'apostles and elders' in 'Jerusalem'. According to the procedure envisaged by Matt. 18:15-18 the local community is in certain cases the final tribunal,[22] and Matt. 23 is directed against an understanding of office and the Church that damages brotherliness.[23]

Hand in hand with the understanding of the community shown by the person in a position of responsibility goes his *understanding of unity*. This too differs in different writings. This can clearly be shown by the image of building that in nearly every passage occurs in the context of unity. In contrast to 1 Cor. 3:9-11, Eph. 2:20-22 and 1 Peter 2:4-8, where the Church is in the process of being built up, we find in 1 Tim. 3:15—'the central ecclesiological passage of the three (pastoral) epistles'—a 'household in which it is a question of living according to fixed rules, according to a domestic routine. . . . Everyone who holds to "sound doctrine" lives in this household, and excluded from it are those who have fallen away into heresy' (2 Tim. 2:20-21). It is a 'firmly . . . established building in which certainty of doctrine and faith is guaranteed. . . . With this a statistical element unmistakeably enters in to the image of the Church'.[24] 'It has consolidated itself and is now concerned to maintain what it has attained, to remain always the same.'[25] What in contrast to this is lacking in the pastoral epistles is the idea of *koinonia* and its dynamic effect.[26] Lacking, too, is the idea of the body of Christ, which provides the basis for a certain necessary pluralism.[27]

Closely connected with the understanding of unity is the idea of *apostolicity*, of great importance for the Church's *search for identity* in the second and third generation of Christians. Apostolicity can be understood in a more open or closed sense. In Ephesians, and in the gospels too, the 'apostles and prophets' (Eph. 2:20, 3:5), the 'disciples' (in the gospels), their faith and their proclamation indicate the unmistakeable 'beginning' (Luke 1:2; 1 John 1:1) or 'foundation' (Eph. 2:20, see Matt. 16:19) as the unsurrenderable *point d'appui* of the Church extending throughout space and time. In the pastoral epistles apostolicity is narrowed down to the single apostle 'Paul'.

3. NORMATIVE PRINCIPLES

The preceding list is not complete,[28] though we must be content with it. In addition, several of the factors mentioned need to be considered in disputes with dissenters.

All the factors mentioned crop up in the later history of the Church when those in positions of responsibility have to deal with dissenters. But that does not yet say anything with regard to the justification of this procedure. Individual facts that can be historically established in the Bible do not in themselves have a normative value just for that reason alone.

On closer examination the factors that have been listed are not specifically biblical or Christian but generally human, sociological and psychological factors that determine the way dissenters are dealt with. These factors can, however, now be investigated for their normative content. Once again there is nothing exceptional about these: they are broadly speaking identical with generally human, sociological and psychological experiences. The order in which they are set out corresponds to that of the factors examined above.

(1) There are greater possibilities of understanding with a peaceful than with a polemical temperament.

(2) A view of the world marked by a concern for wisdom or understood as the history of salvation is more tolerant towards dissenters than a dualistic or apocalyptic one.

(3) A wealth of literary and rhetorical resources offers a dissenter a greater chance of being understood and taken seriously than straight denial, reprimand and the refusal of dialogue.

(4) Theological competence and creativity handle dissenters with more patience than theological incompetence, which has to have recourse to formulas, repetitions and reprimands.

(5) A faith that understands itself as trust and is thus aware that it is sovereign and unmasterable will treat dissenters more generously than a faith that knows its content to be clearly defined.

(6) A living relationship with the community or a good knowledge of the dissenters can indeed entail a more impulsive attitude towards them and for that reason one that is more in keeping with the facts of the case. A more distant attitude to the community and to dissenters can lead to an attitude that is more general but may hide the danger of distorting the dissenters' position.

(7) A differentiated approach to the form and content of the dissenters' demands offers a greater guarantee of a soberly factual controversy than simply treating dissenters as 'opponents'.

(8) The less those in positions of responsibility identify themselves with a particular office within a certain structure, the greater the guarantee that the dispute with dissenters will be conducted with patience.

(9) Where appeal to authority goes hand in hand with competence, the person in a position of responsibility is more likely to do justice to the dissenter than where he relies on a purely external authority.

(10) Someone who is ready to acknowledge a community's maturity and spiritual liveliness is more likely to do justice to dissenters within it than someone who can only give a community little confidence in moral and intellectual matters.

(11) A 'co-operative' understanding of the community is more likely to deal patiently with dissenters than an 'authoritarian' one that thinks of a Church as a pre-determined defined entity.

(12) A dynamic and open understanding of unity is more tolerant towards dissenters than a static or closed understanding of unity that is mainly concerned to hang on to what it has attained and to make it uniform.

4. CONCLUSIONS

It should be pointed out quite clearly that it is not the Bible that establishes the normative principles formulated above but rather that they are established in the Bible.

Individually they are not norms and rules from which a theory of pluralism could be directly derived. Rather they could be regarded as indicative principles which, formulated as firm preferences and taken together, could provide the normative framework for dealing with dissenters. In every case preference would be given to the approach with the greater integrative power. This quality was described in my investigation by such labels as 'ability to understand', 'tolerance', 'taking seriously', 'patience', 'generosity', 'relevance', 'justice', etc. What is striking about this is that these terms provide an approximation to what in the Bible is meant by expressions like *basileia*, *koinonia*, etc. One can also take a sceptical attitude to this indicative filter when it is a question of dealing with dissenters who are bent on obstruction. But the normative framework must above all be maintained in those cases when those in positions of responsibility have to deal with *prophetic dissent*.

It will be up to the systematic branches of theology to investigate these findings with regard to their ethical usefulness.

Translated by Robert Nowell

Notes

1. The passages cited in this study are to be understood as examples. No attempt is made to be exhaustive.

2. For this definition my thanks are due to Dr Max Küchler, whom I would also like to thank here for his many other contributions to this study.

3. On closer examination passages that might seem suited to this turn out not to be. This applies just as much to Matt. 18 as to the pastoral epistles. The procedure outlined in Matt. 18:15-18 is concerned not with a dissenter but with a notorious sinner. As such it is not a question of him justifying himself but of listening—a verb that occurs four times in this short passage. In the pastoral epistles community leaders (Timothy and Titus) are authoritatively instructed how they should deal with dissenters. Meanwhile these instructions cannot be regarded as normative for later ages. Indeed the way in which the struggle against heretics is waged in the pastoral epistles has increasingly been developed by the scholarship of recent years as a reason for denying their Pauline authorship (see the following note). Nor is it clear why the relevant statements of the pastoral epistles should have greater normative value than those of the genuine Pauline epistles.

4. N. Brox *Die Pastoralbriefe* (Regensburger Neues Testament 7/2) (Regensburg 1969) pp. 39-42; W. G. Kümmel *Einleitung in das Neue Testament* (Heidelberg [17]1973) p. 335; P. Trummer *Die Paulustradition der Pastoralbriefe* (Beiträge zur biblischen Exegese und Theologie 8) (Frankfurt-am-Main/Berne/Las Vegas 1978) pp. 161-172.

5. On the subject of Jesus and wisdom, see F. Christ *Jesus Sophia. Die Sophia-Christologie bei den Synoptikern* (Abhandlungen zur Theologie des Alten und Neuen Testaments 57) (Zürich 1970); D. Zeller *Die weisheitlichen Mahnsprüche bei den Synoptikern* (Forschung zur Bibel 17) (Würzburg 1977); M. Küchler *Frühjüdische Weisheitstraditionen. Zum Fortgang des weisheitlichen Denkens im Bereich des frühjüdischen Jahweglaubens* (Orbis Biblicus et Orientalis 26) (Fribourg/Göttingen 1979).

6. H. Schlier *Der Brief an die Epheser. Ein Kommentar* (Düsseldorf 1957) p. 21.

7. W. G. Kümmel, *ibid.* p. 296.

8. Note the contrast with 1 Thess. 2:15.

9. See H. D. Betz 'The literary composition and function of Paul's letter to the Galatians' in *New Testament Studies* 21 (1975) 353-379.

10. Exceptions must always be admitted: Romans 16:17-18.

11. V. Hasler 'Das noministische Verständnis des Evangeliums in den Pastoralbriefen' in *Schweizerische theologische Umschau* 28 (1958) 68.

12. D. Lührmann *Glaube im frühen Christentum* (Gütersloh 1976) p. 30.

13. D. Lührmann, *ibid.* p. 54.

14. K. H. Schelkle *Die Petrusbriefe. Der Judasbrief* (Herders theologischer Kommentar zum Neuen Testament XIII/2) (Freiburg-im-Breisgau 1961) p. 243.

15. G. Lohfink 'Die Normativität der Amtsvorstellungen in den Pastoralbriefen' in *Tübinger theologische Quartalschrift* 157 (1977) 95-101.

16. N. Brox, the work cited in note 4, at p. 226.

17. N. Brox, *ibid.* at p. 176.

18. P. Trummer, the work cited on p. 172: it is only to a limited extent that erroneous doctrine is specifically described in the pastoral epistles.

19. H. Schlier 'Die Ordnung der Kirche nach den Pastoralbriefen' in H. Schlier, *Die Zeit der Kirche. Exegetische Aufsätze und Vorträge* (Freiburg-im-Breisgau ³1962) p. 146.

20. N. Brox, the work cited in note 4, at p. 44.

21. See for example *Kirche im Werden. Studien zum Thema Amt und Gemeinde im Neuen Testament* ed. J. Hainz (Munich/Paderborn/Vienna 1976).

22. W. Trilling *Hausordnung Gottes. Eine Auslegung von Matthäus 18* (Die Welt der Bibel) (Düsseldorf 1960) p. 48: 'The *ecclesia* binds and looses.'

23. H. Frankemölle ' "Pharisäismus" in Judentum und Kirche. Zur Tradition und Redaktion in Matthäus 23' in *Gottesverächter und Menschenfeinde? Juden zwischen Jesus und frühchristlicher Kirche* ed. H. Goldstein (Düsseldorf 1979) pp. 123-189.

24. N. Brox, the work cited in note 4, at pp. 157-158.

25. E. Schweizer *Gemeinde und Gemeindeordnung im Neuen Testament* (Abhandlungen zur Theologie des Alten und Neuen Testaments 35) (Zürich 1959) p. 69.

26. See for example R. Schnackenburg 'Die Einheit der Kirche unter dem Koinonia-Gedanken' in F. Hahn, K. Kertelge, and R. Schnackenburg *Einheit der Kirche. Grundlegung im Neuen Testament* (Quaestiones Disputatae 84) (Freiburg-im-Breisgau 1979) pp. 52-93.

27. 2 Tim. 2:20-21 advocates a rather questionable pluralism.

28. Thus it would be important to look more closely at the sociological status of the group in question, whether their identity is threatened, whether they are threatened from outside, whether they are in danger of falling apart, etc. The situation of the author should also be looked at more closely (imprisonment, persecution, rivalry, etc.). There is much we have not been able to do here, partly for reasons of space, partly because of the difficult position with regard to sources.

Paul Hoffmann

Paul as a Witness to Dissent

1. THE ONE WHO 'DISSENTS' IS THE ONE WHO IS 'CHALLENGED'

IN DEALING with this theme, I have to restrict myself to the quite short period of Paul's activity between A.D. 43 and 56, the period treated, in other words, in the authentic letters. The image of the apostle that is revealed in the Pastoral Epistles is simply that of a 'completed' Paul who was no longer a witness to dissent, but represented 'sound teaching' and a Church that had lost the freedom and dynamism that can legitimately be regarded as characteristic of the historical Paul and the 'Paul' of the 'historian' Luke is no more than a shadow of his former self. The great achievement resulting from the exhausting struggles between the different groups of early Christians was, according to Luke, the single movement that was subjected to the central guidance of the Holy Spirit and the apostles of Jerusalem. Although Paul has for this reason been crowned with the halo of a very successful and powerful missionary, he has at the same time been fitted into this movement without having been given any true theological stature of his own.

These widely accepted images of Paul must certainly be corrected. He was neither the 'prince of the apostles' nor the apostolic 'legate' of a central authority of the early Church. (This function can more suitably be applied to Peter or to Jesus' brother James.) The movement that, with the passage of time, gradually became a monarchical institution in the Church was, during the lifetime of Paul himself, not a single movement, but a pluralistic one, within which certain centres such as Jerusalem and Antioch, where there was scope for individual and group initiatives and independent action, began to take shape. This was partly because there was at that time no central authority that might have been effective in preventing such initiatives.

Paul, who was the exponent of the wing that was directed towards missionising the gentiles, was not only the one who 'dissented', but also the one who was 'challenged' and 'disputed'. Many of those who were no less concerned than he was with the Gospel also regarded him as 'suspect' and 'disreputable'. He had therefore a constant struggle to achieve recognition. This struggle began with his journey to Jerusalem as the representative of the Christians of Antioch, continued throughout the crises in Antioch, Ephesus, Corinth and Philippi and only ended with his last journey to Jerusalem, which was made in the shadow of his defeat in Galatia, so that he had to look for allies among the Christians of Rome (Rom. 15:30f.).[1] The 'danger from false brethren' mentioned in 2 Cor. 11:26 is a clear sign that the history of the Church had begun.

2. ONE AUTHORITY OPPOSED TO ANOTHER

In anathematising or 'cursing' those who were preaching a Gospel that was contrary to the one that he proclaimed in the introduction to his letter to the Galatians, Paul was clearly making full use of his authority against his opponents. It would be quite wrong to identify his anathema with the later form of excommunication practised by the Church. An institutional Church is presupposed by the latter, but Paul is here speaking as one who is conscious of his charismatic and especially of his prophetic gifts and of the effective power of the Pneuma that had been given to him (see, for example, 1 Cor. 5:3-5). His attitude can be compared with that of the early Christian wandering apostles and prophets who pronounced an eschatological curse over the places that rejected them on the basis of the power to bind and loose that was attributed to Peter as a model in Matt. 16:19, but was, according to Matt. 18:18, exercised by the whole community.[2] Paul's consciousness of himself in this role presupposes the charismatic nature of early Christianity, in which it was recognised that certain persons had authority, although that authority was not officially guaranteed, but was based on their own personal vocation and charism.

The Pauline 'curse' has to be applied to Jewish Christian missionaries, who no doubt believed that they were as faithful as Paul himself to the Gospel and who wanted to prevent the Galatians from watering down that Gospel (see Gal. 1:10). Those missionaries called Paul's apostolic authority into question and appealed to the authority of the apostles of Jerusalem. One authority was therefore obviously opposed to another[3] and Paul had to use his skill in argument. He did this with passion and sarcasm. The situation was typical of others in his life. In Antioch, for example, he was opposed to James' people and even to Peter and Barnabas. In Corinth, the conflict broke out first in the community itself—with the members of the community who claimed pneumatic power for themselves and insisted that Paul was in competition with other 'authorities' (see 1 Cor. 1:12). In the final chapters of the second letter to the Corinthians (2 Cor. 11-13), Paul polemically accuses 'super-apostles' and 'servants of Satan' of preaching a different gospel in the community (see especially 2 Cor. 11:4f., 13f.). These were probably wandering apostles of Jewish Christian origin who were charismatically especially gifted.

3. A DECISION IN FAVOUR OF 'PLURALITY'

Gal. 2:1-10 presents us with a conflict from the Antiochian period of Paul. This struggle took place at the so-called 'Apostolic Council' and it is by no means easy to establish the events leading up to it (see, for example, Gal. 2:2; Acts 15:1f.). What is certain, however, is that, according to Paul (Gal. 2:4), some 'false brethren secretly brought in . . . slipped in to spy out the freedom' which the gentile Christians had in Christ. What indisputably happened, then, was that some Jewish Christians, who adhered strictly to the Mosaic Law, were resolutely opposed to the mission to the gentiles, who were not bound by the Law. The Antiochian Christians, with Paul and Barnabas as their spokesmen, continued in the direction in which they had set out and James, the brother of the Lord, Cephas and John, the 'pillars' of the community in Jerusalem, gave them 'the right hand of fellowship' as a sign of their trust and of that fellowship (Gal. 2:9).

Does this incident presuppose the supreme authority of Jerusalem above that of Antioch? The account in the Acts of the Apostles would seem to suggest this and, according to Heinrich Schlier,[4] the statement in Gal. 2:2 can also be interpreted in this sense. Paul says that he 'laid before' the Christians of Jerusalem (in 'care') the gospel that he preached among the gentiles and that he did so 'lest he should be running or had run in vain'. The validity of his gospel seems therefore to have been dependent on Jerusalem. The concluding clause in this verse can, however, also be interpreted as a question: 'whether he should be running . . . in vain', in other words, whether his mission might be unsuccessful. Paul might therefore have seen the justification of the course that he had been following in the success of his mission, which was explicitly acknowledged, at least according to Gal. 2:7f. Even if the first interpretation is preferred, however, neither the preceding statement about Paul's vocation nor the context itself allow us to maintain that the others were, at least according to text itself, subject to the Jerusalem community. The college of three in Jerusalem had only a relative part to play (Gal. 2:6) and it is clear from the account of the way in which unity was reached (Gal. 2:7-10) that a solution to this and other problems could be found by two equal partners.

Nonetheless, Paul respected the Christians of Jerusalem and was concerned that the Gospel should be recognised there. Why is this? It is obvious that he thought of the community in Jerusalem, because of its historical role, as the place where the Gospel had originated and from which the gentile Christians had also received pneumatic gifts (see Rom. 15:27). A breach with Jerusalem would have meant that he had been 'running in vain', even though his gospel derived its legitimacy directly from God, because the fellowship of the Christian communities would have been destroyed and in that fellowship no one partner could succeed without the other.

It is possible that the situation described in 1 Cor. 12 as an interchange between different gifts and ministries in the local community can also be applied to all the Christian communities. If this is so, we have to recognise plurality on the one hand and a willingness to achieve solidarity on the other, not by one partner's supremacy over the other, but by equal and mutual respect. The agreement reached at the Council of Jerusalem represents, in my view, nothing less than a conscious affirmation of that plurality. In recognition of God's effective action, two independent missions were united under the joint authority of Antioch and Jerusalem, although differences remained in theology—they differed, for example, about the status of the Mosaic Law—and each continued to have its own form of organisation and so on. In 1 Cor. 9:19-23, Paul outlined such a programme for himself.[5]

4. CHRISTIAN FREEDOM AND THE TRUTH OF THE GOSPEL

Unity was achieved in Jerusalem, but the Jewish party, with its strict insistence on the Law of Moses, had to pay for it and Paul directed his polemics against the Jewish Christians. Because of material differences, there was clearly no real unity. What was at stake was Christian freedom and the truth of the Gospel (Gal. 2:4f.). For Paul, the two factors belonged together. No compromise was possible where they were concerned. It is interesting to note that this 'truth of the Gospel' was also Paul's criterion for his protest against Peter's attitude (Gal. 2:14) and that, in this case, he was not protesting against a number of extremists, but against his erstwhile partner in Jerusalem and his own community. This brings us to the central question of the theological basis of Pauline dissent.

(a) The Theology of Dissent

The theological presuppositions underlying Paul's argument are disclosed in the passage immediately following the episode concerning Antioch, that is, Gal. 2:15-21. Paul justifies his postulate that we are justified not on the basis of works of the Law, but on faith alone, through the fact that Jesus 'gave himself for me' (verse 20f.) and by the experience of baptism (verse 19). He accepts the soteriology of Jewish Christians of Hellenistic origins (see 1 Cor. 15:3-5; Rom. 3:25f.), but goes beyond the original understanding of this teaching in his interpretation of the forgiveness of past sins by virtue of Jesus' crucifixion as a fundamental overcoming of the concept of justification through the Law (see verse 21).

Very much the same applies to baptism, which Paul interpreted as being saved from the realm of sin and death by a participation in Jesus' resurrection. Paul speaks in this context of dying to the Law (verse 19) and equates being set free from the powers of this world with being set free from the Law in his interpretation of acknowledgment of the Law as a submission to the rule of those wordly powers (Gal. 4:3f., 8-11). Paul takes fully into account the existence of a radical choice between faith and the Law, which originated in his own experience of conversion and was conditioned and determined by his own life. This is clear from Phil. 3, which can be regarded as a key text in the doctrine of justification.

The criticism of Peter is subject to the same presuppositions. The Law has been overcome in Christ and for this reason the Christians of Antioch should not have to submit to Jewish regulations regarding purity. The true meaning of the Gospel is determined by the question of communal meals without observing the Mosaic Law (see Gal. 2:11-14).

(b) The Praxis of Dissent

It is hardly possible to avoid comparing this passage with those texts in which Paul's attitude towards dietary questions in Corinth and Rome is revealed. After scrupulously forbidding the Corinthian Christians to eat flesh offered to idols (1 Cor. 10:14), Paul affirms the position of freedom occupied by the 'strong' in Corinth, but at the same time commits them to respect the consciences of the 'weak' Christians, who might be scandalised by such an emancipated attitude (8:1-13).[6] In the epistle to the Romans, both the 'weak' and the 'strong' have their own right to go their own way and each 'stands or falls before his own master' (see Rom. 14:3f.), but the strong Christian's attitude towards his weaker brethren is, in the letter to the Romans as in the first epistle to the Corinthians, made subject to the criterion of love: 'Do not let what you eat cause the ruin of one for whom Christ died' (14:15; see 1 Cor. 8:11).

Christ's death, then, sets a limit here to Christian freedom and this is justified in the letter to the Galatians, although regard for the brethren of the kind practised by Peter and the Christians of Antioch at the request of the men of James' party would have been understandable. On the one hand, the case for freedom could also have been put forward at Corinth. Was faith in the one God not involved in this restriction of the demand for freedom? Paul decided in favour of freedom in one case and in favour of love in the other. The truth of the Gospel and love for Jesus' sake, the right of Christian freedom and solidarity despite everything with the brethren were all in competition with each other in these concrete situations. In each case, it is true to say that those concerned had to find their own way in a difficult if not insoluble situation.

It has become very obvious in the subsequent history of Christianity that Paul's regard for what would be historically successful was reflected in both of these decisions. *On the one hand, the Church was prevented from following a Judaising tradition and therefore from remaining fundamentally a Jewish sect. On the other hand, however, the Christian understanding of redemption and therefore its concrete relationship with reality were also prevented from being lost in an excessively enthusiastic approach.* In each case, the death of Jesus, as evidence of God's love for *all* men, was the criterion. It was this criterion which prevented Paul from making the salvation of the gentiles dependent on Jewish conditions in his letter to the Galatians. In the epistle to the Corinthians, it caused him to object to a charismatic and enthusiastic understanding of Christianity that overlooked the concrete and historical nature of Christian existence and one's fellow-men.

Paul therefore decided in favour of the poor and underprivileged and against the rich and powerful, in favour of helping and serving one's fellow-men and against special pneumatic gifts, in favour of recognising everyone in the community and against a hegemony of charism and finally in favour of the resurrection of the dead and against redemption seen in purely spiritual terms. The reality of the crucified Christ compelled the Christian community to accept the broken and challenged nature of its historical situation. It called on it to live hoping against hope and not just in looking and contemplating. It outlawed any kind of triumphalism and self-satisfaction in the Church. Paul, in a word, tied the Church firmly down to the cross. A contradiction inspired by Paul has the task of making members of the Church deeply aware of Christ's crucifixion as the ground of Christian freedom and love.

5. SUMMARY

(*a*) Pauline dissent took place—and indeed early Christianity as a whole lived—within an open system with various forms of theology and different kinds of community that were just beginning to emerge. The present question concerning the right to dissent in the Roman Church cannot be isolated from the New Testament. What is required is a critical examination of the prevailing system using the New Testament tradition as a criterion.

(*b*) The plurality of the New Testament tradition leaves ample room for different interpretations of Christian life and praxis, so long as there is total commitment to the fact of Jesus Christ. These varying interpretations may be conditioned by different socio-cultural presuppositions or by the life-style of an individual and Paul is undoubtedly the best example of the latter. Each Christian receives the gift of the Spirit and therefore has the right and duty to follow his own understanding.

(*c*) In the New Testament there is evidence that one apostle or prophet opposed another. Even when Paul, for example, opposed a Christian community on the basis of his own apostolic authority, the truth of the Gospel was never imposed. There was always a need for argument in the interpretation of that truth and it is clear from the New Testament that the better arguments did not always prove to be victorious. Both the unity of the Church and the truth of the Gospel were gained not once but many times in conflicts of interest and differences of opinion. These conflicts and disagreements were in no way exceptional—in deed, they formed an essential part of the social structure of the Church, although it was of fundamental importance that they were resolved in a spirit of free communication and co-operation between equal partners and that a fair balance of interest was achieved.

(*d*) The openness of New Testament Christianity was in danger and that could have led to the Gospel being put at risk. Even during the earliest period of Christianity, Christians who thought differently were branded as heretics and this was, from the historical and sociological point of view, at least relatively right. It is, viewed from one side only, justified as an expression of concern for the truth of the Gospel, at least in so far as that truth was really at stake. It can hardly be justified, however, if branding the other side as heretical resulted in dialogue with that side being broken off and if no arguments were put forward. This praxis cannot even be justified, although there may be evidence of it in the New Testament (see Gal. 1:6-9; 1 Tim. 6:3f., 20f.; Tit. 3:9-11; 2 John 10f.; 3 John 10).

(*c*) The acceptance of an open Church system, which came about as the result of the

Council of Jerusalem, has the unity of the Church as its aim and obliges Christians to work for solidarity. 'Faith working through love' (Gal. 5:6) can never ignore the other person, for whom Jesus Christ died as fully as he died for me. Unity cannot be imposed one-sidedly. It calls for agreement between all the parties concerned and their respect for different points of view. In other words, each side must recognise the Spirit, who is given to everyone in the Church.

Translated by David Smith

Notes

1. See U. Wilckens *Der Brief an die Römer* (Zürich and Neukirchen 1978) pp. 43-46.
2. See P. Hoffmann 'Der Petrus-Primat im Matthäusevangelium' *Neues Testament und Kirche. Festschrift für R. Schnackenburg* (Freiburg 1974) pp. 99-102; F. Hahn 'Der Apostolat im Urchristentum' *Kerygma und Dogma* 20 (1974) 54-77; G. Theissen 'Wanderradikalismus' *Studien zur Soziologie des Urchristentums* (Tübingen 1979) 79-105.
3. For the problem of the 'opponent', see W. Bauer *Rechtgläubigkeit und Ketzerei im ältesten Christentum* (Tübingen ²1964); see also K. Berger 'Die impliziten Gegner' *Kirche. Festschrift für G. Bornkamm* (Tübingen 1980) 373-400, which has recently been supplied with a detailed bibliography.
4. *Der Brief an die Galater* (Göttingen ⁵1971) 68. See also F. Mussner *Der Galaterbrief* (Freiburg 1974) 105; J. Becker *Der Brief an die Galater* (Göttingen 1976) 22; E. Haenchen *Die Apostelgeschichte* (Göttingen ⁷1977) 447-452.
5. H. Conzelmann *Der erste Brief an die Korinther* (Göttingen 1969) 190 says: 'Seen from the point of view of his teaching and from that of the Law, faith and freedom, his attitude is quite consistent. It is that everyone is addressed by God as the man he is, that is, in his *klēsis*. The agreement reached in Gal. 2, that is, that the Jewish Christians should continue to observe the Law, is therefore not a compromise, but a direct application of the concept of *sola fide*.'
6. See G. Theissen 'Die Starken und die Schwachen in Korinth', the article cited in note 2, 272-289.

PART V

Clarifications

José Míguez Bonino

Confrontation as a Means of Communication in Theology, Church and Society

1. THE IDEA OF CONFRONTATION

THE *meaning of the word* ranges from the simple idea of *comparison* (*conferre*) to that of *careo*, as in the right of someone accused to be confronted with his accuser. This is more the sense in which it is to be taken in this study: people opposing one another in opposition, challenge or accusation. In this sense, it implies both a subjective element (two subjects affirming themselves in contradistinction to each other) and an objective one (a content of ideas, principles, programmes or positions in regard to which an opposing stance is taken).

In *sociological theory*, the idea is linked to that of *conflict theory*, which has been widely studied and debated.[1] Coser has distinguished between conflicts 'which do not contradict the basic suppositions on which the relationship is founded' (within a society), and those 'in which the conflicting parties no longer share the basic values on which the legitimacy of the social fabric rests'.[2] Theories that deal with the field of function generally restrict their attention to the first sort, relegating the second to the subjective field of aberrant or deviant behaviour. Logically, this is the view generally taken by those situated in the ruling strata of society, who regard the existing order as normative and can only see conflict as an imbalance or disturbance within the system, which merely requires certain adjustments. From the viewpoint of a critical sociology, on the other hand, although the existence of the first sort of conflicts is recognised, the conflictive nature of society itself is accepted, and deeper conflicts are seen to contain a critical force calling for the transformation of the existing social order. This view is better suited to those who, from a position of oppression or disadvantage, feel the contradictions and failings of the existing system in their own flesh. Since there is no neutral position from which to observe the interplay of social forces, evaluation of conflict and confrontation is inevitably tied to the positions different people hold or assume in society (or in a particular community or institution).

2. THE NATURE AND LIMITS OF CONFRONTATION IN THE CHURCH

The particular nature of the Christian community and of theology makes it impossible to transpose the observations made in the general sociological field directly to confrontation and conflict within the Church and theology. They need to be amended and adjusted on the basis of the characteristics of this community:

(*a*) The Church sees itself as directed towards and participating in an *eschatological end* (the Kingdom of God) which qualifies the conflicts that take place within it. This means that the parties to any conflict have to justify themselves in relation to this end, and prevents any group, section or individual in the ecclesial community from claiming absolute rights. These two aspects are in a continual state of tension. On the one hand, conflicts often tend to 'eschatologise' themselves as matters touching the essentials of faith and to provoke ruptures. On the other, the transcendence of the *'telos'* can often create a wide space for permitted divergences of interpretation and choice, and therefore of conflict and confrontation, which do not lead to breaks. One of the major problems for the Church throughout its history has been distinguishing between one sort of conflict and the other. Furthermore, historical development has shown that conflicts 'absolutised' at one particular moment are later relativised and the groups that have broken apart recognise each other once more and are eventually reunited.

(*b*) A second element stems from the fact that the Church community has a *historical character* which makes it take part in the conflicts and tensions of society (class, race, etc.), while laying claim to a particular character as 'sacrament' of a transcendent reality. In more precise terms, the incarnational nature of Christian faith means that questions relating to transcendence are worked out historically, and that the problems of history always have a dimension of faith. This exposes the Church to two grave dangers. First, the conflicts in society tend to be become sacralised in the Church and to take on the character of 'eschatological wars' with a consequent increase in fanaticism on both sides. Second, matters of faith become 'spiritualised', divorced from actual conditions, leading to an apparent 'peace' or 'unity' which hides the real contradictions inherent in the situation.

Both these dangers need to be taken into account in considering the need for and value of confrontation in the Church, the nature and limits of which need to be measured by these parameters.

3. A TYPICAL NEW TESTAMENT EXAMPLE

Perhaps a brief reference to a typical case of confrontation in the New Testament will help to visualise some of the elements. It is the case of the 'confrontation' (even the original expression κατὰ πρόσωπον αμτῷ ἀντέστην 'I opposed him to his face' in v. 11 gives the same sense word for word) between Paul and Peter described in Galatians 2:11-21. Without going into a detailed study of this, it is worth stressing a few points:

(*a*) The conflict deals with a matter of fundamental importance—'the true meaning of the Good News' (v. 14), the unity of the Church which cancels the distinction between Jew and gentile. But at the same time it refers to a specific agreement made in the Church—what is known as the Council of Jerusalem—which constitutes an immediate ecclesiastical norm mediating that ultimate reality. So the confrontation is necessary in defence of truth and becomes specific in relation to that norm.

(*b*) The verb used, ἀνθίστημι 'to oppose', has the meaning of defending the true *identity* of the Church against a deviation from this.

(*c*) It is difficult to judge the degree of 'rupture' involved in this confrontation. We should perhaps agree with those who see the struggle against the Judaisers as the background to it; Paul saw this as a real betrayal of the Gospel—as 'a different Gospel' (whereas the leaders in Jerusalem had not been able to add anything to his account of the Good News as he preached it to the pagans (v. 6))—and so Peter's 'backsliding' had to be firmly resisted (though still *within the communion* of faith) as it came perilously close to being a different Gospel and threatened to lead others to the same denial of the true meaning of the Good News. What is clear is that there is a decisive qualitative difference between his confrontation with the Judaisers (1:8-9) and his confrontation with Peter.

(*d*) The expression κ.πρόσωπου, 'to his face', indicates a *public* confrontation, as is corroborated by v. 14, 'before them all', which probably took place in the course of an 'assembly'; that is, the conflict was presented to the church community (without questioning the principle of authority). This public nature of the confrontation is worth stressing.

(*e*) Finally, it is interesting to note that the subject matter of the confrontation was a *religious* question with a strong social and cultural content.

I would like now to deal with this type of situation and confrontation, not with the extreme case where it leads to a complete break. Not that extreme cases do not happen, nor that 'intra-communitary' confrontations cannot sometimes take on the nature of crucial divisions in faith. But if we are to consider 'confrontation as *a means of communication*', the emphasis must fall on the type of confrontation that can take place still fully within the Christian community, between subjects who still recognise each other as committed to the same faith and obliged by the same obedience, but who nevertheless oppose their way of interpreting or experiencing this faith (or both) to others which they see as inadequate or even contrary to that faith and obedience.

The limits of confrontation are then set by this recognition (which is sometimes very precarious, as though wrapped in shadows and only perceptible through an act of confidence) that both parties are participating in a common reality; the purpose of confrontation then becomes *to communicate, to convince, to find a common interpretation and practice of this faith*. Is confrontation really a suitable means to achieve this end? Why, and under what circumstances? These questions are not idle or unnecessary, since it is often claimed that confrontation has no legitimate place in the Christian community, that it is basically sterile and contrary to the spirit of the Gospel; and that only dialogue, direct search for a consensus, organic construction of agreement, correspond to the nature of faith. But the biblical models should convince us of the importance of confrontation as a means of communication. Besides the example dealt with here, this subject has been adequately covered in other articles in this issue. Rather than try to justify it here once more on the basis of the Bible, let us seek to establish its value on the basis of the experience of the Church today.

4. DIALOGUE, CONFRONTATION AND POWER

Any relationship between groups of people, inside or outside the Church, has to be seen in its real setting of power relationships. Confrontation becomes necessary when these are such that one of the parties to a dispute holds such a measure of power that he can determine the conditions for and extent of any communication. A typical example—outside the ecclesiastical field—is provided by the *political dialogues* instituted by authoritarian regimes (such as I have come across with a fair number of Latin American military regimes). Here the conditions of dialogue, the forms to be taken by any communication, the limits of any dissension, are all decided in advance, and a monopoly of public information on the course of the dialogue can help to decide even the outcome, which effectively depends on the wish of the power that brings the dialogue about. Under such conditions, dialogue becomes co-option. By accepting it, political groups or parties effectively legitimise a situation over which they have absolutely no effective control. This leaves them with one alternative: unless they can obtain definite guarantees, confrontation is the only way they can stand up for themselves and make their protest public; it is the only way in which they can communicate. *Dialogue as a means of domination is opposed by confrontation as a means of communication.* It would not be hard to find analogies to this situation in the Church.

5. CONFRONTATION AND IDENTITY

A second example, this one taken from the ecclesiastical sphere, will help to clarify another aspect. This is the experience of many churches—and I am referring here to the Protestant ones, since those are the ones I know—which sprang from the missionary endeavours of the North Atlantic churches in what is known as the 'Third World'. When they reach a certain stage in their development, these churches feel the need to deepen their 'indigenisation', but they come up against a *power structure* in which the mother Church, or the missionaries sent out by it, determine the paths of growth, control interpretations, directly or indirectly govern institutions and (consciously or unconsciously) prevent a genuine 'contextualisation', a true meeting of the Church with its people.

In most cases, a simple 'fraternal dialogue' is not sufficient to resolve this situation, because the dialogue is still carried on inside the missionary structures. A confrontation is then needed, which may lead to a demand for a 'moratorium' on the presence of overseas workers and even of aid, or to one for autonomy in administration, theology, liturgy and canon law. The purpose in this case is to create a 'space' in which the local church can develop its own identity. Once this has been obtained—and cases have been known—it is then possible to re-establish dialogue under new conditions: the mother Church acquires a new freedom to be itself, the missionaries can come back and work in freedom, so more effectively, and mutual exchange and enrichment become possible. Confrontation will have been a means for the young church to acquire its own identity and for the mother Church to accede to an authentic dialogue in place of the 'ventriloquism' to which its former domination condemned it.

This need to re-establish a *balance of power* which gives room and allows for the parties in a process of communication to affirm themselves holds good for relations between churches and also for relations within a particular church—between the various individual and collective subjects that make up a church. It applies equally to theological dialogue, since when one form or mode of theology or of 'doing theology'—in our case academic North Atlantic theology, but it can be any other 'canonised school'—backed by ecclesiastical authority or by superior economic and social resources, lays down the canons and directions of theological thought, dialogue is fictitious. Confrontation and in some cases even the refusal to answer (Luke 23:9) can then be a necessary means of establishing a new relationship of authentic and fruitful dialogue.

In Latin America, cultural-religious experience has been particularly dramatic. The policy of 'suppression' of the indigenous population (whether by physical annihilation or by the perhaps even more destructive removal of the economic and social bases of their existence and their cultural means of expression) produced a resistance which took the form partly of imitation and partly of a lapse into the fortress of silence. So, as Dussel has noted, a true dialogue between Christian faith and indigenous culture was made impossible, and therefore there could be no genuine native interpretation of the faith.

This situation has now gone beyond the point at which it can be reversed. But the growth of a 'people's church', which will somehow take on the mantle of this inheritance from the past, offers the only possibility for an 'authentically Latin American Christianity'. This people's church is often forced to confront the ecclesiastical and theological powers in order to win the space it needs to build its identity. Those who see (or want to see) only 'rebellion' or 'disorder' in such manifestations are wrong; these are the conditions needed for articulating oneself as a valid subject—even in order to practise responsible obedience—and so to contribute to a real unity that is not mere domination. The experience of the 'Black church' in the United States is, *mutatis mutandis*, an example of a response to a similar situation. And 'Black theology', with its strong dose of confrontation, has been the means through which this church has been able to 'communicate itself' to the white churches.

6. CONCENTRATION ON DIVISIVE ISSUES

Finally, confrontation is necessary to point out the extreme seriousness of a particular question. I am thinking, to take an example from recent European theological history, of the harsh controversy between Karl Barth and some of his colleagues in the 1930s on the subject of natural revelation. Those who study only the abstract theological content of the debates will not only be astonished at the vehemence of Barth's *Nein*, but will see a need for shades and qualifications of meaning that Barth never looked at. But what was at stake can only be appreciated against the background of the struggle of the Confessing Church. What had to be done in fact, was to cut short any attempt to sacralise possible 'natural' revelations—race, country, culture. What was at stake was the church's freedom to be church. The *confession of faith* in this case has to go through this intransigent exclusivism by which the '*alone*', which in the abstract and in theory would need to be qualified and limited, is the only thing capable of guaranteeing freedom.

Once this critical point has been established and the authenticity of faith safeguarded, then a subtle dialogue in which other points can be recognised and evaluated will become possible. If I understand it correctly, this is the meaning of the intransigence of Latin American liberation theology in insisting on 'the poor' as the only genuine subject and the measure of both theological reflection and ecclesial practice. This is where *authenticity* and *obedience in faith* are judged today. Only a theology and a Church which have made their options clear in the face of this test can legitimately go on to consider other subjects. And for this an 'obstinate', intransigent confrontation is necessary.

Translated by Paul Burns

Notes

1. See the excellent summary in J. Rex *Key Problems in Sociological Theory* (London 1961) chs. 7 and 8.
2. L. A. Coser *The Functions of Social Conflict* (London 1956) p. 151.

Juan José Tamayo-Acosta

The Importance of Organised Opposition Groups and their Rights in the Church

1. THE AUTHORITARIAN NATURE OF THE INSTITUTIONAL CHURCH

ONE OF the most reliable indicators of the degree of flexibility possessed by an institution is its *capacity for tolerance* within its own structure and in relation to other institutions. What often happens is that the originally Utopian and liberating ideals of many movements not only get watered down by power structures, but are even turned into elements used to bolster up the system.

As far as the Church is concerned, it seems to me that the present ecclesiastical apparatus is not only separated chronologically—by almost two thousand years—from the movement represented by those who followed Jesus, but also distanced in kind from the original project set out in the gospels.[1] Throughout its history, the institution of the Church can be said to have been distinguished by the authoritarian, monolithic and intransigent nature of its approach to its internal relationships and to its dealings with society.[2]

(a) Internal Relationships

It has often made use of all sorts of repressive methods to stifle the dissidence of an important sector of its members. Likewise, it has fixed the inheritance received from its founder with unalterable dogmatic rigour where not only doctrine but also discipline and morals are concerned, in such a way as to leave no room for legitimate heterodoxy. Equally, it has appealed to the divine origin of its hierarchical-pyramidal organisation to silence the rich alternative channels put forward by critical Christian groups.

(b) Dealings with Society

Two attitudes have characterised the Church's dealings with society: first, intolerance towards world-views or ideologies differing from its own; second, the religious legitimisation of power structures and thought systems that favoured its privileged position in society.

This double context of intransigence provides the setting in which to understand the importance of opposition movements and organised groups within the Church. Those of us who have experienced our adult Christian faith in a state of permanent conflict with the ecclesiastical institution can only accord such opposition groups a positive and creative value. I would go further: if they did not exist, they would have to be created, since they are as *essential* as the air we breathe if the Church is to recover its evangelical aspect and quite as beneficial in building up the kingdom in its historical phase.

In the present situation, organised opposition groups within the Church are one of the most encouraging signs for the future of Christianity. Without the vehicle of these ecclesial critical groups, those believers who try to live their faith with the clarity required by the times would be unable to be faithful to the Gospel and praxis of Jesus, to the demands of movements for social emancipation, to the continuing achievements of modern society, or to the world of the poor.

Furthermore, such groups and movements are not a novelty of our age, but a constant feature of the history of Christianity.[3] It is only thanks to them that the *prophetic* voice in the Church has been handed on to successive generations, that the origins of the Christian event have been taken as a constant point of reference in theory and in practice, and that bridges of dialogue with other cultures have been built. There is, therefore, a continuous process of opposition that should not be discontinued, and a history that should be kept in mind.

But such movements have all too often been forgotten by the historians of the ecclesiastical 'establishment', their claims ridiculed, their real strength and the extent of their influence played down. This is hardly surprising if one bears in mind that the history of the Church has been written *from within* the official institution and from an orthodox point of view *in order to* justify even the most ignominious actions undertaken against such movements, with a resultant sacrifice of objectivity and academic discipline.[4]

The continuity between past and present ecclesial opposition groups can be seen in a series of attitudes common to all, which can be summed up as follows: community as opposed to individualism and authoritarianism; charism as opposed to legalism; service as opposed to power; Utopia as opposed to the system; horizontal communication as opposed to bureaucracy; participation and coresponsibility valued above centralism; orthopraxis rather than rigid orthodoxy; creativity rather than repetition; festive, outgoing celebration as opposed to formal ritualism; poverty rather than ostentation, etc. This explains both the silence of the historians and the repression to which such movements have been subjected by the ecclesiastical authorities.

2. PLURALISM, CONFLICT AND THE UNITY OF THE CHURCH

One of the distinguishing features of the modern age is its pluralism, that is, 'the present situation in which several world-views hold good for the members of society'.[5] Now this pluralism has also crept into the Church, though belatedly, against a lot of resistance and only to a limited extent. It is a somewhat strange sort of pluralism, which excludes more than it includes, limits more than it broadens. It gives the impression of being just on the surface: 'When Christians, individually or collectively, go beyond the pluralism tolerated by the present ecclesial institution, both as regards their political affiliations and in their interpretation of faith, they come under suspicion'.[6]

But, however one qualifies pluralism within the Church, the fact remains that it has engendered groups and movements opposed to one another and in critical confrontation with the institutional Church. As G. Girardi has written: 'We can see dramatic divisions arising in every sector of Church life. Every country, diocese, parish, movement, religious community, is being torn apart by different tendencies. These divergences affect virtually every question of any importance. In particular, there are certain burning questions in the fields of politics, sexuality and authority, which clearly reveal totally divergent approaches affecting the very meaning of Christianity as a whole.'[7]

Although some condemnatory tendencies still persist in the higher reaches of the hierarchy, opposition groups are today not generally 'officially' judged in terms of heresy or schism. Uniformity is gradually being diluted, the old barriers are being broken down and a new view of the nature of the unity of the Church is emerging.

In the past, the lines drawn between 'good' and 'bad' believers, between those who submitted and the rebels, were drawn according to exact juridical criteria as expressed in canon law. They made it easy to see who was inside and who was outside the Church. The dissidents themselves knew that, if they failed to toe the official line, they would be cut off from the institutional matrix.

Today, however, it does not even occur to the various Christian opposition groups that they might be outside the Church; in general they consider themselves an integral part of the one Church of Christ and they maintain stable relations with other movements of a similar bent and with the institutional Church, even if their relations with the latter are conflictive in character. This conflict turns out to be a necessary ecclesial channel for safeguarding communion. Conflict here does not mean a break, but a fruitful, dynamic and dialectical form of being together, in which the unity of the Church moves through the clear and conscious assumption of conflictivity, and through recognition of the important role played by organised opposition groups within the ecclesial community.

3. WHY DO ORGANISED OPPOSITION GROUPS APPEAR IN THE CHURCH?

While psychological and sociological explanations are certainly enlightening, I do not think they can provide an overall reason for the phenomenon we are studying. We also need to look for explanations internal to faith and the Church. Here I can only give brief notes on the factors that have influenced the inception and consolidation of such groups and movements.

Psychological: Many Christians, unable to feel securely rooted in the present structure of the Church, feeling threatened by its bureaucratic apparatus, create stable opposition groups in which they can find an organisational support for their evangelical crusade.

Sociological: The social pressure exerted by official Christianity in support of dominant interests is still considerable in many countries. This fact has led to the birth of critical Christian groups organised for a double purpose: to counteract this social pressure, and to rediscover the people-liberating dimension of Christianity for the benefit of the most impoverished sectors of society.

Political: The political pluralism found in democratic countries, the currents of dissidence and opposition that appear under dictatorial regimes and the internal pressures within political parties all contribute in a major way to the establishment of opposition groups within the Church and a break with its unfruitful uniformity.

Church institutional: Since Vatican II, a solid movement of criticism of the way the institutional Church works has gathered momentum, aimed at ending the predominance of the institutional aspect of the Church over its communitary aspect. This does not aim at the abolition of the institutional aspect as such, but at a restructuring of it in the light of Jesus' communitary and liberating purpose.

This gave rise to opposition groups and movements dedicated to reformulating the relationships between institution and community, between Church and organisation, between *Church, Kingdom and World*. Today these groups are fighting against three dangers which threaten Christianity:

(*a*) That of identifying the Church with the Kingdom—which presents an idealist image of the Church and one indifferent to historical reality;
(*b*) That of identifying the Church with the World—which projects an image of a secularised Church which fights for power with the secular authorities;
(*c*) That of the Church closing in on itself—which makes it appear self-sufficient and blind to the claims of the secular sphere, the validity of rational discourse and its own mediatory, not absolute, role.

These groups would define the three poles (Kingdom, Church and World) in the following way:

(*a*) The Kingdom as the all-encompassing reality and the final Utopia of the World;
(*b*) The World as the space in which the Kingdom becomes historical and in which the Church is (imperfectly) realised;
(*c*) The Church as mediation of the Kingdom in the World and a historical sign of the Kingdom.

4. THE IMPORTANCE OF CHRISTIAN OPPOSITION GROUPS IN THE CHURCH

There is space here to deal with this final point only in a series of outline propositions, which can perhaps be more fully developed elsewhere:

(*a*) Organised opposition groups and movements within the Church are an *expression of unease* at the way the institutional Church seems to be turning in on itself. A large number of religious men and women live and witness to their faith in such groups. Their exclusion from the Church would mean an impoverishment of the whole ecclesial community.

(*b*) These groups do *not* make up a *parallel Church* to the official one, since their intention is not to break away from it; rather do they work for an alternative of a more evangelical and popular Church. They do, however, have their own organisation and co-ordination, which give them stability and continuity.

(*c*) It follows that these groups are *not sects* made up of pure or 'perfect' believers, but movements set in reality, accepting the challenges of the times and the demands of liberating evangelism.

(*d*) The various organised movements in the Church *cannot be lumped together* or reduced to the tendencies observable in political opposition parties or organisations, since their aim is not to take over power in the Church. All the same, they do share some of the features of political oppositions.

(*e*) The existence of such groups is a *sign of vitality and dynamism* in the Church. They can serve as channels for the most creative energies of Christian faith.

(*f*) Opposition Christian groups are, in their turn, an *organised way* of channelling conflict in the Church. When this is not channelled through well-defined spokesmen, it easily degenerates into a 'wild' destructive confrontation and a sterile splintering.

(*g*) They expose the contradiction apparent in the Church: on the one hand, it preaches a humanitarian and brotherly ideal; on the other, it exists in fact as an institution in which power, learning and possession are unequally divided. Furthermore, these opposition groups tend to go beyond this contradiction in their quest for a *coherent adaptation of the historical embodiment to the brotherly purpose.*

(h) They do *not* aim to take over the positions of the present rulers of the Church through a non-violent *coup d'état*. They rather struggle to give the Church a more dialogal, participative, communitary and democratic structure.

(i) Such groups *are different from the 'Christians without a Church'*, who question radically the possibility of and need for a Church—any church—and opt for living the message of Jesus with no institutional mediation.

CONCLUSION

In view of what has been said, it is not enough to proclaim the right to dissidence in the Church in the abstract, since what usually happens then is that this right is recognised as long as it is not used and withdrawn once it is put into practice. Nor is individual opposition in the person of isolated prophets sufficient—though this does not remove the need for it. The citizens' charter has to be claimed in theory and in practice for organised opposition groups within the Church for the reasons adduced above. This is a modern-day advance as well as a Gospel requirement. Without such a charter we could revert to the days of witch hunts in which not only the prophets but a large number of level-headed believers would also be sacrificed.

This is not a time for excommunications, nor for parallel Churches; it is not the time either for breaks or silent flight. It is time to set the foundations of a different Church that will encourage creativity, respect a maximum of difference within an overall acceptance of the Christian purpose, positively appreciate criticism and foment co-responsibility and a democratic spirit in its bosom.

Basic communities co-ordinated into federations, the 'Christians for Socialism' groups, feminist movements in the Church, groups of critical theologians, and suchlike, form one of the richest assets on which the Church can count for its internal transformation and for the process of making its presence felt in society as servant of the poor.[8]

Translated by Paul Burns

Notes

1. G. Thiessen *Sociología del movimiento de Jesús* (Santander 1979); L. Boff *Eclesiogénesis* (Santander 1979) pp. 68-69.
2. *Mysterium Salutis* IV/I eds. J. Feiner and M. Lohrer; N. Cohn *Los demonios familiares de Europa* (Madrid 1980).
3. N. Cohn *In Pursuit of the Millennium* (London 1979); B. Dunham *Héroes y herejes* (Barcelona 1969) I and II.
4. K. Mannheim *Ideología y utopia* (Madrid 1966). Mannheim claims that in all sociological and historical investigation a vision of the future is operative; this leads him to abandon the ideal of objectivity and impartial research as illusory. The new definition of objectivity he sketches includes the researcher's commitment to the social whole and its transformation. Historical truth only becomes possible through a certain Utopia. In studying opposition movements within the Church, 'confessional' historians will often have offended against this new objectivity.
5. P. Berger *Rumor de ángeles* (Barcelona 1975) p. 81 (*Rumour of Angels*).
6. A. Duran *Iglesia y pluralismo político* (Estella 1976) p. 10.
7. G. Girardi *Cristianismo y liberación del hombre* (Salamanca 1973) p. 179.
8. *Id.*, *Cristianos por el Socialismo* (Barcelona 1977); J. J. Tamayo-Acosta *Comunidades Cristianos populares* (Salamanca 1981).

PART VI

Synthesis

Hermann Häring

The Rights and Limits of Dissent

THE CATHOLIC CHURCH stands, it seems, at the beginning of one of the most difficult phases of its history. For it too is implicated in the new and imponderable *problems of our future*. Since it professes to be 'universal' it manifests more elemental cultural, geopolitical and social oppositions than are to be found elsewhere. It also questions Christian existence, questions how the world can be fashioned in a Christian way. But, more radically than other faith-communities, it can put into play the dynamic energies of new possibilities and impulses within it. The Catholic Church sets an example; consequently the path it takes will be of wide interest.

More decisively than other churches it can hasten the solution of conflicts, occasionally by compulsion; it can apparently eliminate problems through official pronouncements. This makes things difficult, however, for many who are struggling for renewal. Fear of decline and hope of renewal cohabit closely and are seen as being opposed; and the social *stigma of nonconformism* and opposition is experienced and suffered here more consciously than in other Christian communities—and sometimes it is provoked for the sake of a premature unity. Such a marked desire for unity also tends, however, to the fear of diversity and the obstruction of essential experimentation. Thus prophetic inspiration is suppressed by the concern for continuity.

The Catholic Church's opportunity, therefore, is also in danger. Consequently everyone concerned about the Church's future must participate in the dialogue about conflict and its resolution, the rights and limits of dissent. The present issue's contributions have made this clear. They are summarised in what follows; perspectives are drawn and extended and the context of a solution is adumbrated.[1]

1. A HISTORY FULL OF CONFLICT

(a) Fear of conflict

In the Catholic Church conflicts ought to be possible and fruitful. History teaches this. It is not only in the history of Israel—which is also normative for Christians—that a manifold practice of dissent is an *elixir of life* (Murphy); the early Christian communities live with dissent in the most varied ways, gradually becoming reflective (Venetz). Paul, in the struggle between belief in the letter and enthusiasm, persistently voices his dissent and encounters dissent from others. His passion for a solidarity which embraces argument, conceived pluralistically, cuts across all entrenched positions (Hoffmann).

The New Testament canon—marked by the most diverse purposes and situations—opens up a striking plurality of confrontations, soon to be institutionalised in the power of *episcopal and then patriarchal sees*. The history of the Synods of the early Church could substantiate this view. Cyprian's conflict with Rome (Cardman) is thus a representative example showing the role a bishop was able to play at that time, precisely in solidarity with fellow bishops and the Bishop of Rome. Would not Cyprian have paid tribute to our contemporary exercise of episcopacy?[2]

Even today canon law is aware that dissent cannot be calculated or regulated in advance, let alone be dismissed. Thus it indicates judicial and administrative procedures (Provost), the bishops' right of remonstration, provisos in the case of the 'reception' of Church teaching and (of course) conscience. People have become newly aware of the *autonomy of local churches* and the faithful's right to participate in decisions (Huizing/Walf). The unalterable autonomy of different rites and schools (Provost) must be kept in mind, not to mention the independence of an ecclesial theology which, through its method of critical argument which necessarily involves dissent, has always been of service to the open truth of faith.[3] Surely this wealth of experience means that we are on the right track?

The *second millennium*, however, speaks another language. A strengthened papacy tends towards centralism and shows of power. The Waldensians for instance are excluded from the Church contrary to their wishes and convictions; Francis gets into considerable difficulties (Ricca). Other groupings in the middle ages could be adduced.[4] The initial conflict with Martin Luther is taken up as criticism of Church (and papal) authority and thus distorted (Brecht). Thus a spiral of growing *intolerance of dissent* is set in motion. Formally, for instance, Galileo is not condemned on account of astronomical theories but for Church disobedience. This syndrome recurs right up to the most recent disciplinary measures.[5] Surely we should have drawn more profit from the history of the Reformation?

Ignatius of Loyola rightly summons people to *think with the Church*. But this is envisaged hierarchically and above all papally—in fact it implies restriction: 'I will regard what seems white to be as black if the hierarchical Church so decides.' The effects of this spirituality can hardly be overestimated.[6] Finally in the nineteenth century the Catholic Church creates a new, socially embattled identity in which popular veneration of the pope takes on a central role.[7]

Now Rome no longer reacts to conflict and dissent. More and more it makes its own decisions as to where it shall exercise its authority, and assumes a positively *offensive character*. Theologians and churchmen go on the defensive willy-nilly. Teaching authority is subordinated more and more to pastoral authority (Provost). Global confrontations arise such as in the 'Syllabus' of Pius IX (1864); the *magisterium* take the initiative of favouring one theological school (1879); the 'modernist' edifice is destroyed (from 1907)—which, like the doctrine of 'Americanism' (1899), did not really exist as such prior to the papal measures (Daly). This preventive interpretation, blocking the way to new inspirations and for the most part not intrinsic in the events themselves, becomes symptomatic in the course of many conflicts. The spiral of juridism and formalism hardly permits genuine dialogue any more.

Was the Catholic Church unable then to deal with conflict? No, as what followed was to show.

(b) The dynamism of dialogue

For with the Second Vatican Council a path of openness and new communication within the Church had been started, an irreversible process with an inconceivable dynamism—as is the way with all dialogue. For conflicts and dissent which had been banished 'outside' were now brought back into the Church:

—In the *ecumenical dialogue* the problem of unity and dissent becomes a question for self-critical ecclesiology. We see ourselves as unavoidably confronted by the failure of past ages to come to terms with conflict.
—*The dialogue with the 'world'* (with science, cultures, ideologies) confronts us with the problem of truth and error, obliging us to be ready to learn and to engage in continual self-correction.
—*The dialogue with the oppressed* shows us the history of injustice in our own past and presupposes a new scale of values opposed to all 'ecclesiocentrism'.

Objective constellations of problems are treated as being equally as pressing as internal Church conflicts; in a dialogue situation this is necessary and good.

But what, in concrete terms, does this mean? As the contributions of Bonino and Tamayo-Acosta show, the Church's internal *field of force has become fluid*. More than ever, dissent has become a phenomenon of our Church (Provost). The competence of the scientist has become activated along with that of the pastoral worker, the socially involved individual and the 'lay' person who can 'only' draw upon his own experience of faith and of the world. Discipleship of Jesus has once more become an inspiring cause. Against this background the most diverse groups and organised currents, each with their own praxis and interpretation, have come forward demanding a hearing (Tamayo-Acosta). Nowadays unilateral actions on the part of Church leaders often meet with a lively and dissenting echo. People demand reasons. Indeed one cannot grasp all that is going on at the moment on a global scale in the Church.

This background is important for an understanding of our topic. No one should be allowed the right to dissent outside a context of questions of fact and the experience of faith. There should be no legitimation of any and every theological theory or life-style, and there is no question of special rights for theologians, intellectuals or for the Church of a particular country. The traditionally competing claims of Church leadership and theology, of spirituality and reflection, of rational argument and experience, must not be played off against one another. Blank cheques, ultimately pandering to subjectivism and dispensing from brotherly faith-praxis, would be absurd.

(c) **Signs of a new faith-praxis**

We live, however, in a Church in which differences of opinion and dissent are announced on all sides. Mostly they indicate a praxis and a reflection inspired by Christian faith which is beginning to respond to new questions and challenges. This is nothing new in the Church, therefore, but rather the sign of a newly-discovered vitality of which we had been long deprived.

It also means that the Church is beginning, as a community, to face *fundamental contemporary challenges* as well as its own contradictions. As Bonino and Tamayo-Acosta show without difficulty, we are today no longer concerned with defensive dissent. Now the concern is for a new creativity; for faith-experiences, thought-models and social options which have burst the framework of the Church's inherited realisation. The concern is for a new relationship between Church, world and the kingdom of God on the one hand and ecclesial presence and normative origins on the other. The Church itself, as an institution, is committed to the view that it draws its life from charismatic depths; thus it can go beyond itself, in accordance with the Spirit of God, into a new and unknown future.

Dissent, consequently, has adopted a *strategic*, if not offensive *character* in different situations. Liberation theology, feminist theology, Black theology (in its American or African form) and other minority theologies often feel obliged to pursue this path in order to press their cause as Christ's. This fact must be recognised and understood. It is not enough to note the fact of dissent in a particular issue; one must be aware of 'tougher' possibilities—the total context of a strategy of dissent, conscious provocation, the rejection of qualified dialogue (in order to force an unrestricted dialogue), and the refusal of compromise formulas which would obscure central issues. How can we as the Church, how can Church leaders in particular deal with this?

The various contributions have also shown that the question cannot be solved formally. No solution can be said to be found while people are still in dispute with one another. The watchword 'no other Gospel' (see Gal. 1:6)—on the surface not susceptible of dialogue—can signify a *final appeal for communication*. Where people exhibit an eschatological seriousness in the dispute over true discipleship—evoking, naturally, the toughest confrontation—there is always hope of a solution (and to despair of the Spirit of Christ would be utterly un-Christian). Causing uneasiness, the simultaneous 'Yes' and 'No' with regard to a common goal, argument over the right path—all these are once more part of the prophetic medium. It looks as though our Church could be regaining something of its original dynamism and identity. All of us should acknowledge that this hope is worth the cost.

2. FAITH AS THE STRUGGLE FOR REALITY

(a) **No pure community**

We must remember this: none of the familiar internal groupings or movements which go to make up the shape of the Catholic Church today wants to forsake the common *basis of Christian faith*, let alone a lived discipleship. The reverse is for the most part quite tangible. It should not be suggested without solid argument, therefore, that any of them is seeking confrontation for its own sake. None sees itself as an independent ecclesial body, however much it may insist on the dignity of an ecclesial community. In taking on themselves the odium of public dissent in the Church, they are generally striving for a better Church because they have faith in its renewal.

Certainly many critics—even if they had earlier been urging us to clear the decks—see in this process the disintegration of ecclesial unity, the loss of Christian substance, the endangering of faith. All that can be done against such criticism is to clarify the matter at issue and put forward the existential involvement of those concerned. In this issue's contributions it is striking how frank criticism of a particular model of the Church, based on power, goes hand in hand with an unreserved 'Yes' to the community of faith seen as a binding involvement.

There is, however, the much harder, fundamental question as to whether there must be polarisation and conflict at all. Cannot we envisage *a conflict-free Church*? Has not the Catholic Church evolved a strong authority for good reasons? Have not the churches of the Reformation paid for their new path with progressive splintering? Surely dissent has ceased to be legitimate, at the very latest, when the dissenter no longer recognises the unifying basis of the faith?

History, in retrospect, can confirm a theory neither of progress nor of decline.[8] What we must do is acknowledge the dialectic of Christian freedom as well as the *dialectic of ecclesial unity*. Both are committed to a common service (1 Cor. 13). We should not keep trying to establish the pure community, the pure truth, the kingdom of God in some place beyond all conflict. This would be to have exchanged faith's demand, once again, for a morality of bondage and the letter. It would be to have forgotten the Spirit.

(b) Prophetic faith . . .

By contrast, a look at the New Testament shows the Christian message to be more like an expressly *prophetic battle declaration*. The struggle had to take place first within Judaism and then in varied ways within the Church.

Jesus, the bearer of the divine Spirit (Luke 4:18), proclaims more than a religious doctrine: what he wants is a practical response to God's unreserved goodness. He makes this clear by provocations (Matt. 20:15). He illustrates the command of neighbourly love by reference to a heretic (Luke 10:33), the radical nature of conversion by reference to a tax-collector (Luke 18:10) and God's forgiveness in table-fellowship with the unworthy (Mark 2:16). His concern for human beings is enkindled (unnecessarily, one might say) by appeal to the Sabbath commandment (Mark 2:23-28). With his eyes open he sets his face towards Jerusalem. Evidently the kernel of his preaching could only be delivered in prophetic provocation. He preaches the truth of the kingdom in disputes with people, not abstractly. The person who takes the beginning of this kingdom seriously (Mark 1:15) is aiming for the whole, will not tolerate compromise. Not even, perhaps, on the part of the Church's representatives?

In *Paul's* case the question is at once anachronistic and inspiring. Paul was not afraid of open conflict with Peter although he recognised the latter's prominent role (Hoffmann, Bonino). As a theologian he became an exponent of the primitive Church's acceptance of conflict. And not without reason his exemplary confrontation with Peter has always engaged the imagination of theologians.[9] But what do Gospel and kerygma mean for him, and what for Peter? As with many since, part of the acerbity and inevitability of this conflict is due to the fact that the Gospel's bearing on the new questions had not yet been determined, although people had to base their arguments on it.

This hermeneutical problem is a current one. Hence the further anachronistic question as to which side the established theology of the present decades might have taken. Was Paul right in bringing this problem to light or did he exaggerate it? Did he, the 'dissenter', finally set in motion a necessary and decisive process (from the point of view of the new believers) or did he sow the seeds of discord unnecessarily (from the Jewish Christian point of view)? Would not Paul have done better to be humble; would not the problem have been solved more peacefully with different personalities (see Venetz)? Against this background we can put the theological question: Is not the antithesis of law and Gospel part of the message of Jesus Christ, a thorn, a spur to the internal life of the Church? What are the implications for our handling of conflicts?

Paul endeavoured to interpret the message of the cross in the power of the Spirit in terms of the Church's present and future. He became all things to all men (1 Cor. 9:20); that made him vulnerable. Did he always stand firm in the strength of God? This was no more automatic for him (see his 'weakness', 2 Cor. 11) than for *Peter*. Not for nothing does the New Testament exhibit a foil to Paul—by no means an exclusively attractive figure—namely the stereoscopic image of Peter, endowed with grace and yet extremely vulnerable through his breathtaking naivety, at the same time the Rock and the tempting Satan (Matt. 16:18, 22f.), strong in faith yet denying his Lord three times (Luke 22:32, 34), commissioned to 'feed my lambs' and yet earning Jesus' rebuke: 'What is that to you? Follow me!' (John 21:15, 20ff.).[10]

We cannot deduce rules for clearing up problems from such passages. What is crucial is their *spiritual dimension* (1 Cor. 2:13). Consequently they must not be watered down to mere moral exhortation. Rather, they adumbrate the area within which a conflict can be managed in a meaningfully Christian way. This is the spiritual knowledge that every Christian both has rights and yet is vulnerable—and this includes every one of the Church's office-bearers—together with the fundamental Christian experience that we have to strive afresh in each generation to distil the truth of faith from its received form. If the Spirit of Christ wishes to become presence, if he is really to reconcile what is torn by conflict, to free the oppressed, to create friendship; if the kingdom of God is to begin, then the Spirit must apply criticism first of all to those who act in his power; the struggle for a better future must be begun within the Church's own walls.

(c) . . . in the Name of Jesus

Bonino has referred to the particular dangers of such disputes within the Church. But a community which confesses Jesus as Lord has its own specific possibilities. Where it is a matter of concern for man, in God's name, of questioning the path the Church itself is to take, the Church must have recourse, in terms of argument and of life, to the original situation of faith in Jesus Christ. If we confess the presence of Jesus in the Church, if the community of faith is acknowledged to have a positively sacramental character, if the authority of *Jesus' words and deeds* can take us by surprise here and now, calling us to follow him, this recourse must be possible through remembering report, argument, deed and prophetic inspiration.

Doubtless *Paul* expressed this original situation, in the name of the Crucified, in a new way. *Augustine* rediscovered the grace of God which triumphs over everything—albeit against a sombre background. *Waldo* and *Francis of Assisi* tried to put the 'Gospel' into practice in a new freshness (Ricca). And finally *Martin Luther* rediscovered it as the critical measure of the Church (Brecht).

Today it looks as though the faith of Christians has once more found its prophetic inspiration in the contemplation of Jesus of Nazareth. It discovers its original truth in anamnesis and discipleship and, accordingly, responds to the distress of a world which is bent on its own destruction. For from now on, far more than hitherto in a Christendom co-terminous with Europe, what counts is the potential for hope that we can enkindle here and now. The Church which proclaims true doctrine will have to see itself more and more as a community of missionary diakonia.

The foundation text of the traditionally European churches—'He who hears you hears me' (Luke 10:16)—is complemented by a new, church-founding text: 'What you did to the least of these my brethren, you did to me' (Matt. 25:40).[11] The message of the resurrection acquires concrete form as discipleship, as the struggle for *man's humanity*.

Hence we have two criteria: the achieving of a practical hope and recourse to Jesus, the Righteous One before God. The right to dissent must continually justify itself by reference to this content. Under certain circumstances they will *oblige* dissent to be voiced. But is this all?

(d) To realise 'Church' . . .

On the other hand, from a responsibly Catholic viewpoint, any such criteria must be closely examined. We can neither establish a Church of the élite, nor act as though the true Church were only beginning today. In other churches, too, people are becoming aware that it is in the community of faith that we first heard the Christian faith and generally learned how to practise it. Nor can reference to Scripture break this hermeneutical circle, since it is itself the Church's book. And in basing oneself on the Jesus of history one is dependent on accounts which are themselves indisputably indebted to ecclesial presuppositions.[12] So how can anyone undertake to play off Scripture or even Jesus against the Church?

Clear as this argument seems, we must recognise, on the other hand, that it can be abused. It *cannot* be used against the polarisations and instances of dissent within the (Catholic) Church. Here the argument is formal and obscure, and can be reversed in its abstractness: the Church decided in favour of the canonicity of Scripture. It would be positively unecclesial to use it no longer as *norma normous*. And every generation must be confronted afresh with Jesus of Nazareth because the Church *accepts no other Lord* but him. 'Church' seeks realisation as discipleship of Jesus. Otherwise it would no longer be Christian.

Put differently, everything that is 'Church' *wants* to submit itself to the criticism of the Spirit. Any anyone who, on the basis of hermeneutical considerations, involves himself in historical interplay of pre-understanding and critical interpretation, or original question and change of horizon, has all the more reason to look for *new realisations* of Christian living even in (provisional) dissent, indeed, *precisely* there. The Christian message, far removed from any theology of maintaining the status quo in the Church's internal or external relations, calls us all to conversion, including the Catholic Church, on the basis of God's faithfulness.

To reply to particular arguments with calls for an 'ecclesial attitude' is to argue formally; one would first have to prove that these arguments are contrary to Scripture and to Jesus. But to put ecclesiality into practice is to be pursuing the cause of Jesus among men; sometimes, in doing this in a secular and original way, all a person can do is to *affirm* his ecclesiality.

(e) . . . as the locus of dialogue

Does this mean that ecclesiality does not satisfy the necessary criteria? No. But in the dialogue between Church and world, between the various churches and religions, and in the face of world-wide social and political challenge, we need to understand 'Church', too, afresh by going back to its roots in the origin of faith: Church as the *community* of listening, of dialogue, of brotherly support, of communication.[12a] There are references to this in different articles. What is at stake is the fundamental right of all believers to participate in discussion and brotherly correction (Huizing, Walf), more toleration, honesty and flexibility (Provost), a dialogue which is structured and hence facilitated and protected (Stein), the avoidance of any ultimate break (Cardman), the pre-eminence of the Church over its representatives (Brecht), a balance of unity and freedom in love (Daly), a genuine radicalism (Murphy), and the truth of the Gospel in a brotherly community (Ricca).

Venetz measures Church decisions by their *power of integration* and their ability to deal with prophetic dissent productively and by argument. Hoffmann describes Paul's time as the time of an open system with different forms of community and theologies. He points out that unity cannot be achieved by decree. Regarding the present situation Bonino stresses that even a deliberate *confrontation* can be the last chance for dialogue. There are examples of this at the present time. Finally Tamayo-Acosta advocates that organised opposition groups should be given citizenship in the Church. But he does not view opposition as an end in itself, but as the way towards a Church of communication, of mutual respect and of responsibility genuinely shared.

The *hidden question* behind this present issue is therefore this: How can we find and encourage the growth of a brotherly Church, able to promote dialogue and communication? We have not entered here into the dispute over the idea of power-free communication, and for good reasons. Even within the Church, understood as a world-wide organisation, it is not attainable. But it is an idea which applies to the *great Utopia* of Church community, the process of unrestricted exchange. The interaction of the community of believers (articulated in theology in terms of the 'local church') is the source of 'Church'. The latter's eschatological dimension is realised in its experience. As a supra-regional organisation 'Church' is necessarily pluralist; it must be organised by the communities (and groupings) and is dependent upon them for its spiritual life. This is *ecclesiality from below*, therefore, a further criterion of legitimate dissent. It means above all that theory and practice must face up to dialogue and the experience of Christian communities, and must respond to their echo. As in the case of parish leadership, they will not become a law unto themselves and reject dialogue but be candid about their motives, arguments and aims. They will minister to the anamnesis of Jesus as God's Son, which has always been the practice of the assembly of believers.

This done, there would be no further need to quarrel over the rights of co-ordinating organisations, the necessity of all Church institutions, the meaning of administrative oversight, of doctrine and of the preservation of tradition, or even the significance of an authentic corpus of teaching. On the contrary, in a Church community built on primary faith-communities all the energy will be directed towards ensuring that the total community of believers can affirm a common witness. If and when this happens, it will rejoice to be able to speak in the one Spirit. Once more the Petrine ministry would have a unique opportunity, as ecumenical dialogue has shown.[13]

3. ECUMENICAL EXPERIENCE

(a) **Plurality**

Let us return to the question of dissent. It has been shown that dissent will always arise in the Church as a sign of its vitality. But it has also become clear how unprofitable it is to speak in isolation about the rights and limitations of dissent. For its frequency and evaluation, its usefulness or destructive power, whether it has a renewing or merely polarising effect, all this depends on the *openness of the whole system* and its readiness to listen. Evidently, where free communication is possible, personal decision is expected, creative initiatives are regarded as a demonstration of the Spirit, there is a growth in varied and direct dialogue, fruitful provocation and the multiplicity of the gifts of the Spirit. Where communication and participation are repressed by vertical structures[14] relying principally on obedience and authority, bitter opposition, protest and the strategy of disobedience gain the upper hand. Thus the way each age deals with dissent is an indication of its quality of communication.

The first question, therefore, was not 'how should Church leaders react to dissent?'. The question was above all 'What is the total ecclesial context in which dissent can be accommodated; with what model of the Church can we best do justice to the legitimate demands of this phenomenon?'. We can gain a few indications from looking at the problems of ecumenism, within which institutionalised dissent is to be managed.

(i) *Contextuality*

The history of Church divisions and the analysis of the process of divisions shows that contextual dissent is at the root of all major historical disagreements within and between ecclesial communities. Particular doctrines or decisions are at most the precipitating causes; they are not an exhaustive cause of divisions. What is decisive is rather wider cultural, geopolitical, social factors, i.e., a whole context of reality.

Our conclusion is this: dissent which separates churches or threatens unity cannot and must not be reduced to a simple 'Yes' or 'No', ecclesial or unecclesial, Christian or un-Christian. The Christian message must not suppress different social identities but respond to them critically, using the measure of man's humanity. Today, not without reason, the issue is more one of overall convergences, common intentions and motives than one-dimensional differences of doctrine measured in terms of letter and law.

The implication for the Church is this: in the face of serious dissent parish and Church authorities are obliged, to the very best of their ability, to take cognizance of contexts, discover connections and avoid becoming entrenched in letter and law. Convergence must be explored and tested *in mutual respect*. Even when a dialogue breaks down, this horizon which transcends differences in the name of faith must not be forgotten or disavowed.

Conversely there can be a right or *duty to dissent* when there is danger that the (cultural, geopolitical, social) context of a particular group is no longer identified or functioning in a Christian way, but is neglected or even despised. This is where minority theologies and a contemporary missiology (or contextual theology) are vital.[15]

(ii) *Encounter*

The history of mutual rapprochements and unity schemes shows that official dialogues and statements, theological studies and other literature can initiate a new awareness, but this, of itself, does not change the social and *spiritual reality* of different churches. It would be short-sighted to attribute this to the inertia of church-people. Understanding of other faith-communities and groupings can only grow in primary communities of believers through concrete encounters. And only on this basis can a new and comprehensive mutuality of faith and practice develop.

For the Church this implies that, where dissenting groups arise, parish and church authorities have a duty, according to their ability, to create conditions favourable to dialogue, *encounter* and common action. Only in this way can differing contexts be understood and translated, the reciprocal challenge be comprehended and given an expression in terms of *life*. But this can only happen if a readiness is nurtured in ecclesial groups to accept the other as different and allow him an advance of trust. We have a duty to be inquisitive, to undertake spiritual experiments for the sake of the Church's renewal.

Conversely again, there can be the *duty to dissent* in various ways if the structures and fundamental attitudes of a church make such encounters impossible, obstruct translation procedures, discriminate in advance against dissenters. Therefore there must always be discussion about the organisation of churches and the concrete shape of their offices, the right and possibility of public opinion in the Church, and the way faith-communities are actually represented in and by their church administration.

(iii) *Liberation*

Efforts towards a unification of the churches demonstrate, finally, that this process can only be successful if we first devote fresh thought to our missionary, diaconal, world-critical tasks. Churches only come together to the extent that they immerse themselves once more in Jesus' liberating mode of life, a life of dynamism open to the world.

Applied to the problem of dissent this means that Church authorities and ecclesial groupings must measure phenomena of dissent by whether and to what extent they express, in the name of God, the desperate plight of mankind today. For every time dissent is voiced, the dissenter is asked whether he is acting in his own or others' interests. But the believing community and Church authorities must also be asked whether *they* are acting selflessly or egotistically in their dealings with dissenters, however formally 'ecclesial' such dealings may be. Here, too, the right and *duty to dissent* needs to be assessed according to whether the Church is neglecting or even abandoning its task *vis-à-vis* mankind.

Clearly, this third point not only embraces the other two and provides their theme: it touches us today, as ecclesial Christians, on a *sensitive spot*. What political role are the churches playing now that, on the one hand, they have come to see their power in society, and on the other, they have become aware of the problems of our social orders? How can we find our place in this world at a time when we are presenting God's cause with more determination than ever and yet must pursue it as man's cause? Can we solve these problems at all in isolated compartments, or must we not, in order to master the multiplicity of questions, take the long path of *plurality*, both within each church and at the ecumenical level?

Having said this, however, the question remains—are not the criteria we have developed unreal and academic? They are not wrong, but can they be brought to bear? And if such criteria were carried through in practice, would not there be still the need for a final Church authority to decide on the application of the criteria—and hence to decide whether a particular instance of dissent is illegitimate or justified?

(b) Conciliarity

This is a deep and serious question. It contains a specific piece of Catholic Church experience and ecclesial idealism, namely, the hope that unity in Christ will be realised socially. This does not seem to harmonise, however, with that specific area of evangelical experience, according to which faith brings with it a prophetic critique, the dialectic of law and Gospel. Applied to the Church this means that we never finally possess the truth (1 Cor. 13:12). Truth is mirrored in our history. The practical application is that Christian truth is dialogical. Therefore the whole energy of ecclesial truth-seeking must be directed towards seeing *dissent as a contribution to dialogue*, challenge as a possible indication of the Spirit, even disobedience as a form of communication, and to act accordingly. Consequently the primary task of Church authorities must be to lead dissent into dialogue, to promote and safeguard communication and encounter. The Petrine ministry must take care that the Church remains manifold and capable of encounter.

In ecumenical dialogue in recent years the model of a Church uniting along conciliar lines has gained ground.[16] The 'building blocks' of such a Church remain the local communities. Its unity is realised, however, by these local churches being represented (on equal terms) at regional, national and world level. The basis of their reciprocal encounter is dialogue, their principle is the fellowship (including eucharistic fellowship) of all, their goal is to be one in mind. But what motivates them fundamentally is, according to all historical experience, a striving after the cause of Christ.

As a public assembly of the Church deliberating in freedom of speech, therefore, the Council would be the appropriate institution for discovering truth through dialogue, the place where dissent can be changed into dialogue because those who disagree are accepted as brothers and sisters. This would be to have discovered 'bold speech' (2 Cor. 3:12), the only way to achieve consent.

Here we cannot go into the continuity and discontinuity of this idea with the Catholic understanding of the Council, nor the interpretation of Petrine ministry in particular.[17] It is often complemented by the notion of a *'reconciled diversity'*, since we can neither simply ignore denominational differences nor recapture the cultural and ecclesial homogeneity of the early Church. But the basic idea of an unbreakable dialogue-partnership is expressed all the more clearly. The Council's *starting point in dialogue* must be identical with that of the local community, since every baptised person is taught by the Spirit (1 John 2:27). To be consistent, even the Church's conciliar structure should be built up from below. For communication must begin where Christianity can be seen to be credible and livable; it must prove itself on the field of differences and oppositions.

A Church constituted conciliarly could furthermore do the world a *vital service*. If the world needs anything today, it is the example of how to deal successfully with conflicts. It needs the courage to be honest. It needs to hope for prophets who can speak uncomfortable truths. It needs a model; without it, we cannot build a humanity united in peace.

(c) And still dissent?

Will this result in the abolition of all un-Christian dissent? No, as the history of denominations shows. But the question of the rights and limits of dissent would be less distorted. There would be a chance of bringing greater clarity to problems; they would not be tangled up with problems of authority as often occurs now, and the community would find them less of a threat.

Then Bonino's principle could be applied without distortion: *dissent loses its rights when it refuses to be open to dialogue within the Church and explicitly forsakes the common basis of faith and discipleship*. It is illegitimate when it will no longer listen to the consensus of the ecclesial community acting and debating in a Christian spirit. It is at this point, certainly, that Church authorities have a right to declare that the bond of fellowship has been broken—in whatever degree. This was necessary in the early Church; even Paul had to carry it out (Venetz, Hoffmann); and it ought to have occurred in more recent history too (e.g., in the Third Reich).

4. SPIRITUALITY OF DISSENT

No problems have been solved, but a context has been proposed favourable to their solution. Depending upon his point of view the reader may feel that what has been said here shows too much partiality and too little objectivity. Indeed, because of our situation in the Church we were primarily concerned about legitimising dissent, not about its dangers. Many of this issue's contributions are informed by the conviction that the right to speak and reply, the right to voice views publicly, urgently needs strengthening in our Church.

For that very reason we should beware of making dissent into an *end in itself*. The inability to agree is not the same thing as healthy prophecy. Pride ill accords with helpful criticism. They both help to perpetuate a rightly criticised system.

More than ever we need a *common spirituality* of recalling and following Jesus, providing a context for the traditional criteria of authority and obedience. We need a new basis to unite us. We all live 'dangerously', not only those in Church leadership, but also the dissenting groups and their representatives.

Like office-bearers, dissidents are in danger of *isolation*; they both suffer and provoke it. This eliminates any movement towards dialogue, correction and the safety valves of argument and emotional exchange. It encourages dogmatic monologue. So we must always seek dialogue even where it is made so difficult. We need to be questioning, admonishing, pleading; cultivating the art of contact and encounter; in short, we need to be people fit for community.

Like office-bearers, dissidents are in danger of arousing *suspicion* when they criticise. There is an accumulation of negative experiences, a decrease in signs of hope and affirmation. This encourages embittered and non-relevant criticism. Consequently ways must be sought to break the circle of criticism and counter-criticism, initiate forgiveness and a new start, and prosecute the cause of mankind. We need to be people who inspire, who have a vision of the future, promoting trust and creativity; in short, people committed to the future of mankind.

Like office-bearers, dissidents are in danger of the *intolerance* against which they are fighting. Since they are compelled to defend themselves, their own ideas occupy the centre of their thought and activity more and more. This tendency nourishes a self-righteous attitude and results in the loss of Christian balance. We must continually query the Christian substance of what we claim to be the truth. It must be submitted self-critically to the judgment of the Spirit of freedom. We need to be messengers of Jesus and sharers of his destiny; in short, people inspired by Jesus.

Looking to Jesus of Nazareth, then, we must bring affirmation and refutation, mysticism and politics, churchmanship and Christianity into a new relationship. But more than this, we must learn not to be despondent about *our lack of success*. There is a close relation between the ability to accept failure and the relentless pursuit of the cause of Jesus.[18]

Now as always the great *models for dissent* in the Church are the prophets, who could not refute the charge that they were destroying Israel. How could people decide between true and false prophecy on the basis of law and letter (Murphy)? And Paul is the great model for a dissent which could be a constituent characteristic of the Church. Anyone who, as a Christian, has had to adopt the dissenter's role, can find a spiritual treasury not primarily in Galatians but in the dramatic last chapter of 2 Corinthians.

Models for dissent? In conclusion let us recall once again their *Christian prototype*: Jesus of Nazareth, who paid for his protest with a heretic's and insurgent's death. Only against this background can we confess him to be the Risen One and the Son of God. Ever since, dissent in his name has had a unique dignity so long as it follows the words given to Peter: 'Follow me!' (John 21:22).

Translated by Graham Harrison

Notes

1. References to the foregoing contributors are in brackets. For technical reasons they could not all be taken into account.

See *Concilium*: 68 (1971) 'Contestation in the Church' and *Concilium* 88 (1973) 'Polarisation in the Church'. See also K. Rahner 'Schism in the Catholic Church?', 'Heresies in the Church Today?' in *Theological Investigations* 12 (London 1974). The special problem of the authentic *magisterium* in the context of its reception and the apostolic succession is illuminated in *Concilium* 148 (8/1981) 'Who has the say in the Church?'.

2. J. Ratzinger 'Primat und Episkopat' in *Das neue Volk Gottes. Entwürfe zur Ekklesiologie* (Düsseldorf [2]1970). Unfortunately the critical wealth of this approach was never utilised to the full.

3. Pope John Paul II on 15.11.1980 in Cologne: 'The Church desires theological research to be independent and distinct from the Church's *magisterium*, but sharing with it in a common ministry to the truth of faith and the people of God. Tensions and conflicts cannot be avoided. . . . Yet we can always hope that they will be solved in reconciliation if we build on the fact that reason is capable of truth.'

4. H. Grundmann *Ketzergeschichte im Mittelalter* (Göttingen 1963); R. Nelli *Spiritualité de l'hérésie: Le catharisme* (Toulouse 1953); J. B. Russel *Religious Dissent in the Middle Ages* (New York 1971).

5. De Santillana *The Crime of Galileo* (London 1958); *Sonne steh still. 400 Jahre Galileo Galilei* ed. E. Brücher (Mosbach 1964). It is instructive to compare this with the proceedings against H. Küng and E. Schillebeeckx.

6. Rule 13 on the mind of the Church: *Exercises* no. 365; see also Ignatius of Loyola's letter to members of his order in Portugal on 26.3.1553: *Mon. Ign.* 1, IV, 669-681.

7. *Zur Soziologie des Katholizismus* eds. K. Gabriel/F. X. Kaufman (Mainz 1980).

8. H.-J. Schmitz *Frühkatholizismus bei Adolf von Harnack, Rudolph Sohm und Ernst Käsemann* (Düsseldorf 1977); H. Wagner *An den Ursprüngen des frühkatholischen Problems. Die Ortsbestimmung des Katholizismus im älteren Luthertum* (Frankfurt 1973).

9. F. Mußner *Petrus und Paulus—Pole der Einheit. Eine Hilfe für die Kirche* (Freiburg 1976); H. Feld 'Christus, Diener der Sünde'. Zum Ausgang des Streits Zwischen Petrus und Paulus: *Theologische Quartalschrift* 153 (1973) 119-131; see also note 10.

10. H. Küng *The Church* (London 1967) p. 444.

11. J. Moltmann *The Church in the Power of the Spirit* (London 1977) pp. 126-130.

12. E. Schillebeeckx *Christus und die Christen* (Freiburg 1977) pp. 58-71.

12a. L. Boff *Die Neuentdeckung der Kirche. Basisgemeinden in Lateinamerika* (Mainz ²1980) pp. 9-21.

13. *Papsttum als ökumenische Frage* (Munich-Mainz 1979); W. Kasper 'Dienst und der Einheit und Freiheit der Kirche. Zur gegenwärtigen Diskussion um das Papsttum in der Kirche' in *Catholica* 32 (1978) 1-23; see the eagerly-awaited final document of the Anglican-Roman Catholic International Commission (ARCIC), 'Authority in the Church II', published earlier this year.

14. M. Hermanns *Kirche als soziale Organisation. Zwischen Partizipation und Herrschaft* (Düsseldorf 1979); see on a key problem in this context: 'Electing our own Bishops' *Concilium* 137 (7/1980).

15. W. Bühlmann *Wo der Glaube lebt. Einblicke in die Lage der Weltkirche* (Freiburg 1974); F. Faucher *Acculturer l'évangile: mission prophétique de l'Église* (Montreal 1973); D. J. Hesselgrave *Communicating Christ Cross-Culturally* (Grand Rapids ³1980); *Your Kingdom Come. Mission Perspectives. Report on the World Conference on Mission and Evangelism 1980* (Geneva 1980); this publication reports on a number of conflict theologies.

16. H. Meyer ' "Einheit in versöhnter Verschiedenheit"—"konziliare Gemeinschaft"— "organische Union". Gemeinsamkeit und Differenz gegenwärtig diskutierter Einheitskonzeptionen' in the last publication cited in note 15, at 377-400; J. R. Nelson 'Konziliarität—Konziliare Gemeinschaft' in *Ökumenische Rundschau* 27 (1978) 358-377.

17. H. Küng *Strukturen der Kirche* (Freiburg ²1962); W. Beinert 'Konziliarität der Kirche. Ein Beitrag zur ökumenischen Epistemologie' in *Catholica* 33 (1979) 81-108.

18. A. Houtepen 'Koinonia and Consensus. Towards Communion in One Faith' in *Sharing in one hope. Bangalore 1978* (Geneva 1978) 205-208.

Contributors

JOSÉ MÍGUEZ BONINO was born in Argentina in 1924 and studied theology in Argentina, the USA and Holland. He is an ordained minister of the Evangelical Methodist Church of Argentina, and has been a President of the World Council of Churches as well as visiting professor in the USA, England, Rome and Strasburg. His works include the following in English or translated into English: *Doing Theology in a Revolutionary Situation* (1975), *Christians and Marxists* (1975), *Room to be People* (1979), and a chapter 'A View from Latin America' in *Agenda for Prophets* (1981).

MARTIN BRECHT was born at Nagold in West Germany in 1932. He studied theology at the universities of Tübingen and Heidelberg, gaining his doctorate in 1961 and his qualification as a university lecturer (*Habilitation*) in 1965. Since 1975, he has been professor of Church history in the department of Protestant theology at Münster University. His publications include: *Die frühe Theologie des Johannes Brenz* (1966), *Martin Luther. Sein Weg zur Reformation* (1483-1521) (1981) and numerous articles on the history of the Reformation in the seventeenth and eighteenth centuries, which have appeared in *Archiv für Reformationsgeschichte*, *Zeitschrift für Kirchengeschichte* and *Blätter für württembergische Kirchengeschichte*. He has also edited *Theologen und Theologie an der Universität Tübingen* (1977), *Text—Wort—Glaube. Festschrift für Kurt Aland* (1980). He was co-editor of *Bekenntnis und Einheit der Kirche. Studien zum Konkordienbuch* (1980) and *Verkündigung und Forschung—Pietismus und Neuzeit, Jahrbuch zur Geschichte des neueren Protestantismus*. His editions include: *Johannes Brenz, Werke* (1970ff.) and *Philipp Matthäus Hahn, Tagebücher* (1979ff.).

FRANCINE CARDMAN is associate professor of historical theology at Weston School of Theology in Cambridge, Massachusetts. She did her doctoral work at Yale University in historical theology and patristics, with a dissertation on Tertullian. Her translation of Augustine's *De Sermone Domini in Monte* was published as *The Preaching of Augustine*, ed. J. Pelikan. Her research and teaching interests include the history of spirituality, patristics, ecumenism, and feminist theology. She is currently president of The North American Academy of Ecumenists.

GABRIEL DALY was born in Dublin, Eire, in 1927. He entered the Augustinian Order in 1944, and was ordained priest in 1951. He gained an STL at the Gregorian University, Rome, an MA in history at Oxford University and a PhD in theology at Hull University. He teaches systematic and historical theology at the Milltown Institute of Theology and Philosophy, the Irish School of Ecumenics, and Trinity College, Dublin. He has published *Transcendence and Immanence: A Study in Catholic Modernism and Integralism* (Oxford 1980), and has contributed chapters to *Irish Anglicanism* ed. M. Hurley (Dublin 1970), *Witness to the Spirit* ed. W. Harrington (Dublin 1979), *Understanding Human Rights* ed. A. Falconer (Dublin 1980). He also contributes articles and reviews to *The Irish Theological Quarterly*, *The Heythrop Journal*, etc.

HERMANN HÄRING was born in 1937 and is married. His principal areas of interest, in research and publications, are Christology, dogmatics, ecclesiology and ecumenical questions. Since 1980 he has been professor of dogmatic theology at the Catholic University of Nijmegen.

PAUL HOFFMANN was born in 1933, studied theology in Paderborn, Munich and Münster, became a doctor of theology in 1959, was ordained priest in 1961, qualified as a university lecturer in 1968 and since 1970 has been professor of New Testament studies at Bamberg University. His publications include: *Die Toten in Christus. Eine religions-geschichtliche und exegetische Untersuchung zur paulinischen Eschatologie* (Münster 1966, ³1978), *Studien zur Theologie der Logienquelle* (Münster 1972, ³1982), written in collaboration with V. Eid, *Jesus von Nazareth und eine christliche Moral. Sittliche Perspektiven der Verkündigung Jesu* (Freiburg 1975, ³1979), 'Auferstehung der Toten/Auferstehung Jesu Christi' *Theologische Realenzyklopädie* 4 (Berlin 1979) 450-467, 478-513, ' "Er weiss, was ihr braucht . . ." (Mt. 6, 7). Jesu einfache und konkrete Rede von Gott' *Stuttgarter Bibelstudien* 100 (Stuttgart 1981) 151-176, 'Eschatologie und Friedenshandeln in der Jesusüberlieferung' *Stuttgarter Bibelstudien* 101 (Stuttgart 1981) 115-152.

PETER HUIZING, SJ, was born in 1911 in Haarlem, joined the Society of Jesus in 1931 and was ordained priest in 1941. He studied at the universities of Amsterdam, Nijmegen and Louvain and at the Gregorian University in Rome, is a licentiate in philosophy and theology and emeritus professor of canon law in Nijmegen. Professor Huizing was a consultor on the papal commission for the reform of canon law. His publications include: *Schema structurae iuris canonici matrimonialis* (1963), *De Trentse huwelijksreform* (1966), 'Um eine neue Kirchenordnung', in Müller, Elsener and Huizing *Vom Kirchenrecht zur Kirchenordnung?*

ROLAND E. MURPHY, OCarm, is the George Washington Ivey professor of biblical studies at Duke University (Durham, NC). He is the co-editor and contributor for *The Jerome Biblical Commentary*, and he has written many studies on biblical subjects.

JAMES PROVOST was born in 1939 in Washington, DC. Ordained a priest at Louvain (Belgium) for the diocese of Helena, Montana (USA), he gained a doctorate in canon law at the Lateran University in Rome in 1967. He served as chancellor and officialis of the diocese of Helena from 1967 to 1979, and currently serves as associate professor of canon law at the Catholic University of America. President of the Canon Law Society of America in 1977-78, he is now executive co-ordinator of the Society and directs its permanent seminar on research in canon law and theology. He is managing editor of *The Jurist* and edits the *Proceedings* of the Canon Law Society of America. He has published various articles on canon law and on pastoral issues.

PAOLO RICCA was born in 1936 at Torre Pellice (Turin). He studied theology in Rome and Basel, where he obtained a doctorate. Consecrated priest in Waldensian Church in 1962, he did pastoral work till 1976, and since 1976 has been professor of Church history and practical theology at the Waldensian faculty of theology in Rome. His publications include: *Die Eschatologie des vierten Evangeliums* (1966), *Il cattolicesimo del Concilio* (1966), *La 'morte di Dio: una nuova telogia?* (1967), *Il cristiano davanti all a morte* (1978), *Pietro e il papato nel dibattito ecumenico odierno* (in collaboration with Bruno Corsani) (1978).

ALBERT STEIN was born in 1925 at Cleves in West Germany, but now lives in Vienna. He was a judge in various courts in Germany, ending his career as a lawyer in Cologne. From 1971 onwards, he taught theology and from 1976 onwards was professor of practical theology, specialising in Church order, in the faculty of Protestant theology at Bonn University. Since 1 January 1978, he has been president of the Institute for Church Law in the faculty of Protestant theology at Vienna University, where he is also a professor. Among his publications are: *Probleme evangelischer Lehrbeanstandung* (Bonn 1967), *Evangelische Laienpredigt* (Göttingen 1972), *Evangelisches Kirchenrecht. Ein Lehrbuch* (Neuwied 1981). He has also contributed to the *Evangelisches Staatslexikon* (Stuttgart and Berlin ⁷1975), the *Evangelisches Soziallexikon* (Stuttgart and Berlin ⁷1980), the *Theologische Realenzyklopädie* (Berlin) and has written articles, from 1970 onwards, on Protestant Church law, especially for the *Zeitschrift für evangelisches Kirchenrecht* (Tübingen).

JUAN JOSÉ TAMAYO-ACOSTA was born in the province of Palencia in Spain in 1946. He holds a doctorate in theology from the Pontifical University of Salamanca and a diploma in social sciences from the Leo XIII Institute, and at present teaches theology at the University Institute of Theology and the Centre for University Studies in Madrid. He is co-editor of the ecumenical review *Pastoral Popular*. His books include *El asalto a la fe* (1977), *Un projecto de Iglesia para el futuro en España* (1978), and *Comunidades Cristianas populares* (1981).

HERMANN-JOSEF VENETZ, born in 1938 at Brig, Switzerland, obtained his licentiate in biblical studies at Rome and his doctorate of theology at Fribourg. Since 1975 he has been professor of New Testament exegesis at the theological faculty of Fribourg University. He is president of the Swiss Catholic Biblical Society. His publications include: *Die Quinta des Psalteriums. Ein Beitrag zur Septuaginta—und Hexaplaforschung* (Collection Massorah I/2) (1974), *Der Glaube weiss um die Zeit. Zum paulinischen Verständis der 'letzten Dinge'* (Biblische Beiträge 11) (1975), *So fing es mit der Kirche an. Ein Blick in das Neue Testament* (1981).

KNUT WALF was born in Berlin in 1936 and ordained priest in 1962. He studied philosophy, theology, jurisprudence and canon law in Fribourg and Munich, gaining his doctorate and *Habilitation*. From 1966 to 1968 he did pastoral work in West Berlin. In 1972 he was appointed university lecturer in canon law and civil law relating to the Church and in 1974 he joined the board of the university's institute of canon law. Since 1977 he has been professor of canon law at the University of Nijmegen. His publications, apart from articles and contributions to collections, include: *Die Entwicklung des päpstlichen Gesandschaftswesens in dem Zeitabschnitt zwischen Dekretalrecht und Wiener Kongress (1159-1815)* (1966), *Das bischöfliche Amt in der Sicht josephinischer Kirchenrechtler* (1975), *Menschenrechte in der Kirche* (1980).

CONCILIUM

1. (Vol. 1 No. 1) **Dogma.** Ed. Edward Schillebeeckx. 86pp.
2. (Vol. 2 No. 1) **Liturgy.** Ed. Johannes Wagner. 100pp.
3. (Vol. 3 No. 1) **Pastoral.** Ed. Karl Rahner. 104pp.
4. (Vol. 4 No. 1) **Ecumenism.** Hans Küng. 108pp.
5. (Vol. 5 No. 1) **Moral Theology.** Ed. Franz Bockle 98pp.
6. (Vol. 6 No. 1) **Church and World.** Ed. Johannes Baptist Metz. 92pp.
7. (Vol. 7 No. 1) **Church History.** Roger Aubert. 92pp.
8. (Vol. 8 No. 1) **Canon Law.** Ed. Teodoro Jimenez Urresti and Neophytos Edelby. 96pp.
9. (Vol. 9 No. 1) **Spirituality.** Ed. Christian Duquoc. 88pp.
10. (Vol. 10 No. 1) **Scripture.** Ed. Pierre Benoit and Roland Murphy. 92pp.
11. (Vol. 1 No. 2) **Dogma.** Ed. Edward Schillebeeckx. 88pp.
12. (Vol. 2 No. 2) **Liturgy.** Ed. Johannes Wagner. 88pp.
13. (Vol. 3 No. 2) **Pastoral.** Ed. Karl Rahner. 84pp.
14. (Vol. 4 No. 2) **Ecumenism.** Ed. Hans Küng. 96pp.
15. (Vol. 5 No. 2) **Moral Theology.** Ed. Franz Bockle. 88pp.
16. (Vol. 6 No. 2) **Church and World.** Ed. Johannes Baptist Metz. 84.pp.
17. (Vol. 7 No. 2) **Church History.** Ed. Roger Aubert. 96pp.
18. (Vol. 8 No. 2) **Religious Freedom.** Ed. Neophytos Edelby and Teodoro Jimenez Urresti. 96pp.
19. (Vol. 9 No. 2) **Religionless Christianity?** Ed. Christian Duquoc. 96pp.
20. (Vol. 10 No. 2) **The Bible and Tradition.** Ed. Pierre Benoit and Roland E. Murphy. 96pp.
21. (Vol. 1 No 3) **Revelation and Dogma.** Ed. Edward Schillebeeckx. 88pp.
22. (Vol. 2 No. 3) **Adult Baptism and Initiation.** Ed. Johannes Wagner. 96pp.
23. (Vol. 3 No. 3) **Atheism and Indifference.** Ed. Karl Rahner. 92pp.
24. (Vol. 4 No. 3) **The Debate on the Sacraments.** Ed. Hans Küng. 92pp.
25. (Vol. 5 No. 3) **Morality, Progress and History.** Ed. Franz Bockle. 84pp.
26. (Vol. 6 No. 3) **Evolution.** Ed. Johannes Baptist Metz. 88pp.
27. (Vol. 7 No. 3) **Church History.** Ed. Roger Aubert. 92pp.
28. (Vol. 8 No. 3) **Canon Law—Theology and Renewal.** Ed. Neophytos Edelby and Teodoro Jimenez Urresti. 92pp.
29. (Vol. 9 No. 3) **Spirituality and Politics.** Ed. Christian Duquoc. 84pp.
30. (Vol. 10 No. 3) **The Value of the Old Testament.** Ed. Pierre Benoit and Roland Murphy. 92pp.
31. (Vol. 1 No. 4) **Man, World and Sacrament.** Ed. Edward Schillebeeckx. 84pp.
32. (Vol. 2 No. 4) **Death and Burial: Theology and Liturgy.** Ed. Johannes Wagner. 88pp.
33. (Vol. 3 No. 4) **Preaching the Word of God.** Ed. Karl Rahner. 96pp.
34. (Vol. 4 No. 4) **Apostolic by Succession?** Ed. Hans Küng. 96pp.
35. (Vol. 5 No. 4) **The Church and Social Morality.** Ed. Franz Bockle. 92pp.
36. (Vol. 6 No. 4) **Faith and the World of Politics.** Ed. Johannes Baptist Métz 96pp.
37. (Vol. 7 No. 4) **Prophecy.** Ed. Roger Aubert. 80pp.
38. (Vol. 8 No. 4) **Order and the Sacraments.** Ed. Neophytos Edelby and Teodoro Jimenez Urresti. 96pp.
39. (Vol. 9 No. 4) **Christian Life and Eschatology.** Ed. Christian Duquoc. 94pp.
40. (Vol. 10 No. 4) **The Eucharist: Celebrating the Presence of the Lord.** Ed. Pierre Benoit and Roland Murphy. 88pp.
41. (Vol. 1 No. 5) **Dogma.** Ed. Edward Schillebeeckx. 84pp.
42. (Vol. 2 No. 5) **The Future of the Liturgy.** Ed. Johannes Wagner. 92pp.
43. (Vol. 3 No. 5) **The Ministry and Life of Priests Today.** Ed. Karl Rahner. 104pp.
44. (Vol. 4 No. 5) **Courage Needed.** Ed. Hans Küng. 92pp.
45. (Vol. 5 No. 5) **Profession and Responsibility in Society.** Ed. Franz Bockle. 84pp.
46. (Vol. 6 No. 5) **Fundamental Theology.** Ed. Johannes Baptist Metz. 84pp.
47. (Vol. 7 No. 5) **Sacralization in the History of the Church.** Ed. Roger Aubert. 80pp.
48. (Vol. 8 No. 5) **The Dynamism of Canon Law.** Ed. Neophytos Edelby and Teodoro Jimenez Urresti. 92pp.
49. (Vol. 9 No. 5) **An Anxious Society Looks to the Gospel.** Ed. Christian Duquoc. 80pp.
50. (Vol. 10 No. 5) **The Presence and Absence of God.** Ed. Pierre Benoit and Roland Murphy. 88pp.
51. (Vol. 1 No. 6) **Tension between Church and Faith.** Ed. Edward Schillebeeckx. 160pp.
52. (Vol. 2 No. 6) **Prayer and Community.** Ed. Herman Schmidt. 156pp.
53. (Vol. 3 No. 6) **Catechetics for the Future.** Ed. Alois Müller. 168pp.
54. (Vol. 4 No. 6) **Post-Ecumenical Christianity.** Ed. Hans Küng. 168pp.
55. (Vol. 5 No. 6) **The Future of Marriage as Institution.** Ed. Franz Bockle. 180pp.
56. (Vol. 6 No. 6) **Moral Evil Under Challenge.** Ed. Johannes Baptist Metz. 160pp.
57. (Vol. 7 No. 6) **Church History at a Turning Point.** Ed. Roger Aubert. 160pp.
58. (Vol. 8 No. 6) **Structures of the Church's Presence in the World of Today.** Ed. Teodoro Jimenez Urresti. 160pp.
59. (Vol. 9 No. 6) **Hope.** Ed. Christian Duquoc. 160pp.
60. (Vol. 10 No. 6) **Immortality and Resurrection.** Ed. Pierre Benoit and Roland Murphy. 160pp
61. (Vol. 1 No. 7) **The Sacrame Administration of Reconcilia** Ed. Edward Schillebeeckx. 160pp.
62. (Vol. 2 No. 7) **Worship of Christian Man Today.** Ed. Herman Schmidt. 156pp.
63. (Vol. 3 No. 7) **Democratizat of the Church.** Ed. Alois Müller. 160pp.
64. (Vol. 4 No. 7) **The Petrine Ministry in the Church.** Ed. Hans Küng. 160pp.
65. (Vol. 5 No. 7) **The Manipul of Man.** Ed. Franz Bockle. 144pp.
66. (Vol. 6 No. 7) **Fundamenta Theology in the Church.** Ed Johannes Baptist Metz. 156p
67. (Vol. 7 No. 7) **The Self-Understanding of the Church.** Ed. Roger Aubert. 144pp.
68. (Vol. 8 No. 7) **Contestation the Church.** Ed. Teodoro Jimenez Urresti. 152pp.
69. (Vol. 9 No. 7) **Spirituality, Public or Private?** Ed. Chris Duquoc. 156pp.
70. (Vol. 10 No. 7) **Theology, Exegesis and Proclamation.** Roland Murphy. 144pp.
71. (Vol. 1 No. 8) **The Bishop a the Unity of the Church.** Ed Edward Schillebeeckx. 156p
72. (Vol. 2 No. 8) **Liturgy and Ministry.** Ed. Herman Schm 160pp
73. (Vol. 3 No. 8) **Reform of th Church.** Ed. Alois Müller a Norbert Greinacher. 152pp.
74. (Vol. 4 No. 8) **Mutual Recognition of Ecclesial Ministries?** Ed. Hans Küng Walter Kasper. 152pp.
75. (Vol. 5 No. 8) **Man in a Ne Society.** Ed. Franz Bockle. 160pp.
76. (Vol. 6 No. 8) **The God Question.** Ed. Johannes Bap Metz. 156pp.
77. (Vol. 7 No. 8) **Election-Consensus-Reception.** Ed. Giuseppe Alberigo and Ant Weiler. 156pp.
78. (Vol. 8 No. 8) **Celibacy of t Catholic Priest.** Ed. William Bassett and Peter Huizing. 160pp.
79. (Vol. 9 No. 8) **Prayer.** Ed. Christian Duquoc and Clauc Geffré. 126pp.
80. (Vol. 10 No. 8) **Ministries ir Church.** Ed. Bas van Iersel Roland Murphy. 160pp.
81. **The Persistence of Religion.** Andrew Greeley and Grego Baum. 0 8164 2537 X 168pp
82. **Liturgical Experience of Fai** Ed. Herman Schmidt and D Power. 0 8164 2538 8 144pp
83. **Truth and Certainty.** Ed. Edward Schillebeeckx and E van Iersel. 0 8164 2539 6 14
84. **Political Commitment and Christian Community.** Ed. A Müller and Norbert Greinac 0 8164 2540 X 156pp.
85. **The Crisis of Religious Lang** Ed. Johannes Baptist Metz Jean-Pierre Jossua. 0 8164 2541 8 144pp.
86. **Humanism and Christianity.**

Claude Geffré. 0 8164 2542 6 144pp.
The Future of Christian Marriage. Ed. William Bassett and Peter Huizing. 0 8164 2575 2.
Polarization in the Church. Ed. Hans Küng and Walter Kasper. 0 8164 2572 8 156pp.
Spiritual Revivals. Ed. Christian Duquoc and Casiano Floristán. 0 8164 2573 6 156pp.
Power and the Word of God. Ed. Franz Bockle and Jacques Marie Pohier. 0 8164 2574 4 156pp.
The Church as Institution. Ed. Gregory Baum and Andrew Greeley. 0 8164 2575 2 168pp.
Politics and Liturgy. Ed. Herman Schmidt and David Power. 0 8164 2576 0 156pp.
Jesus Christ and Human Freedom. Ed. Edward Schillebeeckx and Bas van Iersel. 0 8164 2577 9 168pp.
The Experience of Dying. Ed. Norbert Greinacher and Alois Müller. 0 8164 2578 7 156pp.
Theology of Joy. Ed. Johannes Baptist Metz and Jean-Pierre Jossua. 0 8164 2579 5 164pp.
The Mystical and Political Dimension of the Christian Faith. Ed. Claude Geffré and Gustavo Guttierez. 0 8164 2580 9 168pp.
The Future of the Religious Life. Ed. Peter Huizing and William Bassett. 0 8164 2094 7 96pp.
Christians and Jews. Ed. Hans Küng and Walter Kasper. 0 8164 2095 5 96pp.
Experience of the Spirit. Ed. Peter Huizing and William Bassett. 0 8164 2096 3 144pp.
Sexuality in Contemporary Catholicism. Ed. Franz Bockle and Jacques Marie Pohier. 0 8164 2097 1 126pp.
Ethnicity. Ed. Andrew Greeley and Gregory Baum. 0 8164 2145 5 120pp.
Liturgy and Cultural Religious Traditions. Ed. Herman Schmidt and David Power. 0 8164 2146 2 120pp.
A Personal God? Ed. Edward Schillebeeckx and Bas van Iersel. 0 8164 2149 8 142pp.
The Poor and the Church. Ed. Norbert Greinacher and Alois Müller. 0 8164 2147 1 128pp.
Christianity and Socialism. Ed. Johannes Baptist Metz and Jean-Pierre Jossua. 0 8164 2148 X 144pp.
The Churches of Africa: Future Prospects. Ed. Claude Geffré and Bertrand Luneau. 0 8164 2150 1 128pp.
Judgement in the Church. Ed. William Bassett and Peter Huizing. 0 8164 2166 8 128pp.
Why Did God Make Me? Ed. Hans Küng and Jürgen Moltmann. 0 8164 2167 6 112pp.

109. **Charisms in the Church.** Ed. Christian Duquoc and Casiano Floristán. 0 8164 2168 4 128pp.
110. **Moral Formation and Christianity.** Ed. Franz Bockle and Jacques Marie Pohier. 0 8164 2169 2 120pp.
111. **Communication in the Church.** Ed. Gregory Baum and Andrew Greeley. 0 8164 2170 6 126pp.
112. **Liturgy and Human Passage.** Ed. David Power and Luis Maldonado. 0 8164 2608 2 136pp.
113. **Revelation and Experience.** Ed. Edward Schillebeeckx and Bas van Iersel. 0 8164 2609 0 134pp.
114. **Evangelization in the World Today.** Ed. Norbert Greinacher and Alois Müller. 0 8164 2610 4 136pp.
115. **Doing Theology in New Places.** Ed. Jean-Pierre Jossua and Johannes Baptist Metz. 0 8164 2611 2 120pp.
116. **Buddhism and Christianity.** Ed. Claude Geffré and Mariasusai Dhavamony. 0 8164 2612 0 136pp.
117. **The Finances of the Church.** Ed. William Bassett and Peter Huizing. 0 8164 2197 8 160pp.
118. **An Ecumenical Confession of Faith?** Ed. Hans Küng and Jürgen Moltmann. 0 8164 2198 6 136pp.
119. **Discernment of the Spirit and of Spirits.** Ed. Casiano Floristán and Christian Duquoc. 0 8164 2199 4 136pp.
120. **The Death Penalty and Torture.** Ed. Franz Bockle and Jacques Marie Pohier. 0 8164 2200 1 136pp.
121. **The Family in Crisis or in Transition.** Ed. Andrew Greely. 0 567 30001 3 128pp.
122. **Structures of Initiation in Crisis.** Ed. Luis Maldonado and David Power. 0 567 30002 1 128pp.
123. **Heaven.** Ed. Bas van Iersel and Edward Schillebeeckx. 0 567 30003 X 120pp.
124. **The Church and the Rights of Man.** Ed. Alois Müller and Norbert Greinacher. 0 567 30004 8 140pp.
125. **Christianity and the Bourgeoisie.** Ed. Johannes Baptist Metz. 0 567 30005 6 144pp.
126. **China as a Challenge to the Church.** Ed. Claude Geffré and Joseph Spae. 0 567 30006 4 136pp.
127. **The Roman Curia and the Communion of Churches.** Ed. Peter Huizing and Knut Walf. 0 567 30007 2 144pp.
128. **Conflicts about the Holy Spirit.** Ed. Hans Küng and Jürgen Moltmann. 0 567 30008 0 144pp.
129. **Models of Holiness.** Christian Duquoc and Casiano Floristán. 0 567 30009 9 128pp.
130. **The Dignity of the Despised of the Earth.** Ed. Jacques Marie Pohier and Dietmar Mieth. 0 567 30010 2 144pp.
131. **Work and Religion.** Ed. Gregory Baum. 0 567 30011 0 148pp.
132. **Symbol and Art in Worship.** Ed. Luis Maldonado and David Power. 0 567 30012 9 136pp.
133. **Right of the Community to a Priest.** Ed. Edward Schillebeeckx and Johannes Baptist Metz. 0 567 30013 7 148pp.
134. **Women in a Men's Church.** Ed. Virgil Elizondo and Norbert Greinacher. 0 567 30014 5 144pp.
135. **True and False Universality of Christianity.** Ed. Claude Geffré and Jean-Pierre Jossua. 0 567 30015 3 138pp.
136. **What is Religion? An Inquiry for Christian Theology.** Ed. Mircea Eliade and David Tracy. 0 567 30016 1 98pp.
137. **Electing our Own Bishops.** Ed. Peter Huizing and Knut Walf. 0 567 30017 X 112pp.
138. **Conflicting Ways of Interpreting the Bible.** Ed. Hans Küng and Jürgen Moltmann. 0 567 30018 8 112pp.
139. **Christian Obedience.** Ed. Casiano Floristán and Christian Duquoc. 0 567 30019 6 96pp.
140. **Christian Ethics and Economics: the North-South Conflict.** Ed. Dietmar Mieth and Jacques Marie Pohier. 0 567 30020 X 128pp.

1981
141. **Neo-Conservatism: Social and Religious Phenomenon.** Ed. Gregory Baum and John Coleman. 0 567 30021 8.
142. **The Times of Celebration.** Ed. David Power and Mary Collins. 0 567 30022 6.
143. **God as Father.** Ed. Edward Schillebeeckx and Johannes Baptist Metz. 0 567 30023 4.
144. **Tensions Between the Churches of the First World and the Third World.** Ed. Virgil Elizondo and Norbert Greinacher. 0 567 30024 2.
145. **Nietzsche and Christianity.** Ed. Claude Geffré and Jean-Pierre Jossua. 0 567 30025 0.
146. **Where Does the Church Stand?** Ed. Giuseppe Alberigo. 0 567 30026 9.
147. **The Revised Code of Canon Law: a Missed Opportunity?** Ed. Peter Huizing and Knut Walf. 0 567 30027 7.
148. **Who Has the Say in the Church?** Ed. Hans Küng and Jürgen Moltmann. 0 567 30028 5.
149. **Francis of Assisi Today.** Ed. Casiano Floristán and Christian Duquoc. 0 567 30029 3.
150. **Christian Ethics: Uniformity, Universality, Pluralism.** Ed. Jacques Pohier and Dietmar Mieth. 0 567 30030 7.

All back issues are still in print and available for sale. Orders should be sent to the publishers,

T. & T. CLARK LIMITED
36 George Street, Edinburgh EH2 2LQ, Scotland